CHRIST'S WAY OF AFFIRMATION

EMBRACING ALTRUISTIC AFFIRMATION
ESCAPING FOOLISH FLATTERY

Trust in the Lord -

R. Samaan

PHILIP G. SAMAAN

Books by Philip G. Samaan

Christ's Way to Pray
Christ's Way to Restoration
Christ's Way of Reaching People
Christ's Way to Spiritual Growth
Christ's Way of Making Disciples
Portraits of the Messiah
Blood Brothers

To order: Call (423) 236-2982

or E-mail: pgs@southern.edu

CHRIST'S WAY OF AFFIRMATION

EMBRACING ALTRUISTIC AFFIRMATION
ESCAPING FOOLISH FLATTERY

PHILIP G. SAMAAN

Copyright © 2011 by
Philip G. Samaan
All rights reserved

The author assumes full responsibility for the accuracy of all facts and quotations as cited in this book.

Unless otherwise indicated, Bible texts in this book are from the New King James Version. Copyright © 1979, 1980, 1982 by Thomas Nelson, Inc. Used by permission. All rights reserved.

Cover designed by Brian Wiehn
Layout design by Frank Strack

Typeset: 11.25/14.25 Bembo

PRINTED IN U.S.A.

07 06 05 04 03   5 4 3 2 1

ISBN 0-9824395-1-2

Printed by College Press LLC
Collegedale, Tennessee

Dedication

Dedicated to Jesus Christ
The perfect Example of genuine affirmation

Contents

Introduction

In a culture that focuses on individualism and self reliance, it is not easy to know how to give or receive a genuine compliment. Oftentimes we wonder if it is proper to give such a compliment to someone for fear of it coming across as flattery. You would agree with me that on some occasions you may have heard the recipient of a well-meaning compliment respond: "Flattery will do you no good." You remember thinking at such instances that you were misunderstood, unappreciated, or that even your motives were misconstrued. There is among us a misunderstanding as to what constitutes a genuine, well-deserved compliment meant to encourage and affirm, as contrasted with empty and insincere flattery. The first is meant to affirm in the Lord, the latter is insincere and is intended to deceive, manipulate, and build up one's ego.

It happens sometimes when offering a sincere and appreciative compliment to a pastor for his helpful sermon, or a musician for her inspiring piece that we get this response: "It wasn't that good; I didn't have much time to prepare." What is this response supposed to mean? It could possibly imply a posture of humility, pride, or an amalgamation of the two. It could also reveal discomfort with any affirming comments. Those being complimented maybe want to give the impression that with only a little preparation they apparently can do so well, but imagine how much more they could do if they had the chance to prepare well for the occasion.

There are also the extremes of avoiding giving any compliment for fear of engendering pride: "We don't want it to go his head." Or there are the unwarranted compliments for no matter what for the supposed enhancement of self-esteem. Why can't the beneficiaries of an encouraging sermon or an inspiring musical rendition just say that they are thankful to the Lord for the blessings received through their ministry? And why can't public presenters simply respond by saying that they are grateful to God for using them to bless others? That would be a win-win situation: The Lord would be given praise and glory, the public presenters would be affirmed in Jesus, and the affirmers would feel appreciated.

Of course, there are plenty of empty flattery and false compliments practiced by people-pleasers. Such employ this approach to mislead and manipulate others for one's own benefit, under the guise of supposed kindness and friendliness. God condemns such false pretensions uttered by flattering tongues. He associates this evil practice with ungodliness, unfaithfulness, idleness, and double-mindedness. "Help, Lord, for the godly man ceases! For the faithful disappear from among the sons of men. They speak idly everyone with his neighbor; with flattering lips and a double heart they speak. May the Lord cut off all flattering lips and the tongue that speaks proud things" (Ps. 12:1-3). Public flattery is common and it conveys a certain impression about someone, but it is rare to hear one-on-one affirmation.

Some caution is here warranted relating to counterfeits of genuine affirmation. We live in an age in which obsession with self-worth has been beaten into people's psyche. Under the illusion of enhancing self-worth, deceptive compliments are lavishly heaped on anyone without rhyme or reason. This enables children as they grow up to become spoiled, self-indulgent, and proud. A youngster scribbles a few crooked lines in his school notebook, and shows it to his dad in trying to get his attention. Dad hastens to say that it is a wonderful drawing. His son retorts that it takes him only a few seconds to purposely do some careless scribbling, and that his work is in no way a piece of art. "But it is," the father protests. "Son, everything you do is great!"

But there is the clear danger that in going to the extreme of not seeming to flatter, that we miss out on being Christlike in genuinely affirming others. There is a vacuum in the human heart for genuine compliments, sincere commendations, and enabling encouragements; a vacuum of not only how to graciously receive but how to graciously give as well. No wonder Victor Hugo asserted that "man lives by affirmation, even more than by bread." And Mark Twain expressed a similar idea when he testified that he could "live for two months on one good compliment." It is essential to keep in mind that whatever good gifts God desires to bestow upon us, Satan has his counterfeits. He cleverly counterfeits genuine affirmation that brings glory to God, with false flattery that brings conceit to man.

Even though we will have a whole chapter in this book on the evils of flattery, drawing a sharp distinction between that and altruistic affirmation, yet we are not going to dwell on the deceiver's counterfeits but on Christ's example of affirmation. In this way we will not be in danger of taking extreme positions in this important area of human experience: either avoiding the needed ministry of genuine affirmation, or sliding into the pit of flattery and people-pleasing. We will explore together how Jesus affirmed people of different walks of life, how He lifted up their spirits, and inspired hope in them to live for

Him. There is so much tearing down of people, why not build them up in Christ? There is a great hunger for the ministry of affirmation in the body of Christ today. What is implied in our key word "affirmation" is the idea of encouragement, validation, recognition, appreciation, commendation, valuing, and support.

Let us keep in mind as we proceed on this exciting quest that altruistic affirmation is in the heart of Jesus for each of us. Flattering adulation is never Christ's way of treating anyone. Here is what altruistic affirmation means:

- To make firm something true, to positively assert the good in someone.

- To reinforce something worthy of regard and appreciation.

- To confirm someone in his God-given gifts and qualities.

- To value, validate, support, strengthen, and uphold someone in Jesus.

- So, let us then embark on this exciting journey of affirmation, moving forward in Christ's name, and becoming more like Him in this crucial area of human relationships.

CHAPTER ONE

Divine Affirmation

"And suddenly a voice came from heaven, saying,
'This is My beloved Son, in whom I am well pleased'"
(Matthew 3:17).

After several counseling sessions, a well-educated and cultured professional confided in me that the most painful hindrance and stifling influence in his life was his inability to please his perfectionist father. Try as he may to accomplish this life-long goal of his, he never arrived. Even at his father's deathbed, as he breathed his last, he never said to his son that he was pleased with him. Bitter disappointment filled his heart knowing that he had lost his last chance at pleasing his dying father. He was afraid that this disappointment would stay with him all his life.

I had the chance to share with him my own experience in my younger years of not arriving at pleasing my heavenly Father. Personally, it was more crucial to please my heavenly Father, though my earthly father was pleased with me. What concerned me were the issues of salvation, sanctification, and being ready for Christ's coming. What finally helped him was what helped me years ago when I experienced the joy and peace of knowing that my heavenly Father was well pleased with me. Why was I so sure of that? Because He was well pleased with Jesus who was covering me with His own righteousness. When we talk about His divine pleasure with us because of His Son Jesus, we are talking about the pleasure of the perfect One, absolutely perfect in every way. If the sovereign King of the universe is pleased with us because we are submitted to Jesus, then this awesome reality must liberate us from any anxiety of being good enough to please anyone.

I further explained to this man that whenever I read the affirming words of the Father to His Son in Matthew 3:17, I felt somewhat excluded. After all, His wonderfully reassuring words were spoken to His absolutely perfect Jesus not to poor imperfect me, or was it? O how much I wanted to please my heavenly Father! But it seemed that the harder I tried to please Him, the harder it was for me to experience His divine pleasure in my life. I often pondered what it would take to hear His affirming words, "You are My beloved son in whom I am well pleased," said about me. I wondered if I could dare contemplate such a glorious prospect. Who was I to even think that God would ever actually be pleased with me as He was pleased with Jesus?

Divine Adoption

Then I was led to the encouraging promise found in Ephesians 1:5, 6. There in verse five we are promised divine adoption as sons and daughters of the King through Jesus Christ our elder Brother. And when we open our hearts and fully embrace this divine adoption into Christ's family, our heavenly Father is pleased with us. Then in verse six we are told the tremendous news that by God's grace "He has made us accepted in the Beloved." Wholeheartedly embracing Christ the Beloved Son of God, we are embraced and accepted as His beloved children.

In looking up the comments in *The Desire of Ages*, page 113, I was struck with this amazing assurance which made it abundantly clear that I may, by His grace, fulfill the ardent desire of my heart. My great desire was to hear my heavenly Father say to me what He said to Christ that I was His beloved son in whom He was well pleased. Here is the statement: "The glory that rested upon Christ is a pledge of the love of God for us.... By sin, each was cut off from heaven, and alienated from its communion; but Jesus has connected it again with the sphere of glory. His love has encircled man, and reached the highest heaven. The light which fell from the open portals upon the head of our Savior will fall upon us as we pray for help to resist temptation. *The voice which spoke to Jesus says to every believing soul, This is My beloved child, in whom I am well pleased"* (emphasis supplied).

The idea of affirmation is enshrined in the heart of God from eternity, and Jesus came to reveal His Father's heart to us. In the Messianic prophecy found in Isaiah 7:14 we read that Jesus' name would be called Immanuel. And shortly before Jesus was born, the angel of the lord announced this good news about Him: "And she will bring forth a Son, and you shall call His name Jesus, for He will save His people from their sins" (Matt. 1:21). Here we have two names for Jesus whose meaning and significance is full of divine affirmation to sinful humanity. The name "Immanuel" refers to God being with us, and the name "Jesus" signifies that God saves. In other words, God in Christ is with us in order to save us.

Love Seeks Togetherness

So, in spite of all our human sinfulness and degeneration, Jesus ardently desires to be with us. Genuine love seeks togetherness, and that is why the "Word became flesh and dwelt among us" (Jn. 1:14). He loves us for sure, because He desires our company. Moreover, He is with us not merely for fellowship but also for salvation. He is available as our Immanuel, and He is able as our Savior. Regardless of how worthless or hopeless we see ourselves, He comes to us garbed in our humanity, affirming us that we are worth His fellowship and salvation.

Christ's Way of Affirmation

There are many misconceptions as to why Jesus came to live among us. Why was God willing to give His only Son to helpless and hopeless humanity? Many feel that God views them in terms of His arbitrary justice, judgment, and condemnation. But John 3:16 and 17 tells us the real reason for Christ's divine mission. Heaven could not keep Him away from our pathetic plight, because He loved us regardless, came to save us from our sins, and to restore us unto Himself. God so loved everyone in the world to the extreme extent of giving up His only Son. What great affirmation that He loved us *as much as* His own unique and beloved Son! And this inestimable love was manifested through His death for us while we were yet sinners and enemies.

He Desires Everyone to Be Saved

Everyone, without exception, is predestined to be saved by this tremendous sacrifice of love. "Whosoever believes in Him should not perish" implies that anyone, everyone, and all who accept and appropriate His gift of salvation shall be saved. What a great encouragement to believe that God through His Son is on our side—He is not against us, He is indeed for us. He "desires all men to be saved and to come to the knowledge of the truth" (1 Tim. 2:4). And He is "not willing that any should perish but that all should come to repentance" (2 Pet. 3:9). According to our Lord no one ever has to perish, because He desires, predestines, and wills you and me not to be condemned, but to be saved. Yet in His love and sovereignty He allows us the freedom to choose or reject such a great salvation. He desires our salvation, but we need to join His desire; He wills our redemption, but we need to submit our will to His.

Our loving heavenly Father, in His innermost being, is definitely not in the business of condemnation but in the sacred mission of salvation. He "did not send His Son into the world to condemn the world, but that the world through Him might be saved" (Jn. 3:17). Lost people have nothing to fear from Christ their Savior, for all the authority and power of Heaven is at His disposal to rescue them. The big question is: are they willing to be rescued and be restored? Christ desires to uphold and strengthen us through His solid promises as He did in affirming repentant Zacchaeus in Luke 19:10. Jesus said that, "the Son of Man has come to seek and to save that which was lost." For Christ to seek in order to save lost human beings, whom He created and redeemed, does not by any means signify condemnation but points clearly to affirming support.

Divine Inclusion

In His support and affirmation, Jesus is long-suffering with us, patiently waiting for His empowering grace to effect transformation. Although the disciples still had lingering doubts and ongoing struggles, yet Christ shared with them His Father's divine affirmation. This is nowhere articulated more clearly than in John 17. Here are some of these encouraging words of divine inclusion that we can apply to our daily lives as we walk with Jesus:

1. He is glorified in us. Just think of the enormous implication to us: when we follow Him, the eternal Son of God, He is actually glorified in our faithfulness to Him and His mission (v. 10).

2. He wants His joy to be fulfilled in us. That eternal and profound joy that Christ set before Him (Heb. 12:2) in saving lost humanity, He wants to share with us as we join Him in saving others (v. 13).

3. He sanctifies Himself for our sake. Christ commits and consecrates Himself for His sacred mission of redemption, that He may draw us to Himself so that we may be

sanctified by the glorious truth of the gospel (v. 19). It is such a source of great encouragement that the King of the universe is so committed to us and to our close relationship with Him.

4. He desires us to be one with Him and the Father. He longs to share with us this intimate fellowship with His Father. He wants to be included and to belong to this complete circle of divine-human fellowship. It is way beyond any human imagination to fathom such great love, intimate unity, and divine fellowship, yet our Lord wants us to be a part of it all (v. 23). In John 15:15 Jesus wants to call us His friends, taking us into His confidence, and sharing with us the secrets of His heart and kingdom. What an awesome compliment that He thinks so well of us and has such high hopes for our relationship with Him.

5. Finally, He longs to have us behold His glory face-to-face when He comes again to take us unto Himself. Think of the great hope He has for us: to be always in His presence, and to gaze at His glory forever (v. 24).

Genuine Friendship

To cap all these wonderfully affirming words of Christ to us, let us contemplate more of what He says in John 14:3. "And if I go and prepare a place for you, I will come again and receive you to Myself; that where I am, there you may be also." Genuine friends enjoy keeping in touch, and enjoy dropping by and visiting in each others' homes. They enjoy each other's company. Now Jesus is our most wonderful Friend and Bridegroom, and He is eagerly waiting to take us unto Himself to celebrate the wedding feast of the Lamb with us. All is ready for the reception: our wedding celebration and our eternal home. This will be our eternal abode where we will be with Jesus as His beloved bride. How Jesus views us should fill our hearts with perpetual wonder and tremendous encouragement. His affirmation is so overwhelming in that He ardently desires to be with us for ever as His precious bride.

There is no more precious gift that we can bestow on our loved ones and friends than the gift of time and togetherness. Parents may lavishly provide all sorts of gifts to their children except the most important one: quality time. Often the material gifts overshadow the giver, but the giver is the most important gift. Gifts are not an end in themselves, but point us to God the Giver. You see, time is life, and investing time in them is investing of one's life, which is the highest expression of love. This investment of life in another outweighs by far all material gifts. One is profound and enduring; the other shallow and temporary.

Heart and Life Investment

Jesus provides the supreme example of life-investment—all-embracing and everlasting. He invested His life on the cross for our sake, thus retaining humanity in His being forever. Imagine with me for a moment how infinitely affirming it is to humanity for the eternal Son of God to irrevocably alter His divine nature. Before His incarnation He was fully divine, but after His incarnation He also became fully human, thus linking Himself with humanity with a bond that would never be broken. The redeemed will forever have this unique relationship with Jesus that will be the perpetual study of the entire universe. The focus of universal attention will be on Jesus and us who have gone through such a matchless divine-human experience. There is absolutely no other real source of affirmation and self-worth than how Jesus views us and relates to us. Why not wholeheartedly embrace this divine affirmation and be full of His courage, hope, and strength?

Christ's Way of Affirmation

A young lady came to my office to talk to me about her homesickness, living away from home for the first time. She confided that she particularly missed her dad. She was grateful that he had showered her with all that she needed for college: a car, laptop computer, money, and so on. But what she needed most from her dad—time to get to know him, to communicate with him heart-to-heart—he seemed unable to provide. Her good father was able and willing to give anything she wanted, except the gift of himself. She explained to him that before going on her own, she desired that they get to know each other on a deeper level and enjoy a close father–daughter relationship. She particularly felt the need to reach out to him in that way, because she knew that after leaving home this bonding would become unlikely. The independence of adulthood, career, marriage, and children awaited her. All he could say was that the university had good counselors to help her with her problem. But her desperate need was not really that of a counselor but of a father, and not a problem to be solved, but a relationship to be established and nurtured.

How grateful we ought to be for the way our heavenly Father yearns to relate to us. Grateful that through Jesus He longs to have an intimate, heart-to-heart relationship. With His big heart He unfailingly takes the initiative to make such a quality relationship a reality, for now and forever. When Jesus comes again He will give great commendations to those who were faithful to Him and His service. "Well done, good and faithful servant; you were faithful over a few things, I will make you ruler over many things. Enter into the joy of your Lord' (Matt. 25:21). This is indeed a most affirming commendation. And to hear these approving words at the end of our faithful labor is most reassuring.

"It is the faithfulness, the loyalty to God, the loving service, that wins the divine approval. Every impulse of the Holy

Spirit leading men to goodness and to God is noted in the books of heaven, and in the day of God the workers through whom He has wrought will be commended" (*Christ's Object Lessons*, p. 361). Moreover when we enter into the joy of our Lord in heaven we will sit at the banqueting table spread before us to celebrate the marriage feast of the Lamb. The high honor and the great divine approval will take place when our Lord, the Bridegroom Himself, will serve us. The Master will serve the servants! In prefiguring the final reward, Jesus said: "Blessed are those servants whom the master, when he comes, will find watching. Assuredly, I say to you that he will gird himself and have them sit down to eat, and will come and serve them" (Lk. 12:37).

DISCUSSION QUESTIONS

1. What is the best thing that we can do to experience God's great pleasure towards us?

2. What is the meaning of the names "Jesus" and "Immanuel," and how does that reveal God's divine affirmation toward fallen humanity?

3. Expound on the statement that genuine love seeks togetherness. What does this tell you about Christ's regard toward us?

4. As you contemplate Christ's five affirming references to His disciples in John 17, which is your favorite one, and why?

5. Why will the redeemed in heaven be God's show case for the entire universe to study and marvel at?

CHAPTER TWO

Affirming Children

"And Jesus called a little child to Him, set him in the midst of them, and said, 'Assuredly, I say to you, unless you are converted and become as little children, you will by no means enter the kingdom of heaven'"
(Matthew 18:2, 3).

O nce we paid a visit to a family to congratulate their little boy on his birthday. He was turning four that day, and was pleasantly surprised to see his pastor and wife come especially to visit him. The parents thought we had come to visit the grown-ups, but we explained to them that their precious child was a very important little member of our church family. Giving him a gift and a card, I remember setting him on my lap and gently enfolding him in my arm, and attentively listening to all he wanted to say about his special day. As time came to say good-bye, I bent down to his level, took his face into my hands, looked into his eyes and said that Jesus loved him a lot, and I loved him too and was very happy to have him in our church. Then I prayed a short prayer for him, thanking Jesus for His special gift of another year of protection and happy life. For years the parents would tell me the positive spiritual impact this visit had on their child as he was growing up.

As God's Spirit moves upon my heart, I try to emulate Christ's example in relating to children. I want them to grow up associating the Christian life with something loving and real.

By the way I treat them I desire that they be drawn toward Christ by love, not repulsed from Him by indifference. After all, the children are the future of our church, society, and our nation. It is really the greatest investment we can pour our hearts into, returning great dividends. Whenever the opportunity presents itself, I receive great rewards from taking time from my hectic schedule to talk to children, laugh and play with them. It is really mutually beneficial because they get encouraged, and I unwind from the difficult problems I have to deal with, and let go of them.

The Lover of Children

Can you imagine Jesus welcoming the innocent and trusting company of children in order to relieve His soul from the treachery of the Pharisees? His bitter opponents tried to constantly make His human journey trying and difficult. His enemies' suspicions, accusations, raging anger, and murderous conspiracies vexed His heavy heart. "Jesus was ever a lover of children. . . . Their grateful praise from their pure lips was music in His ears, and refreshed His spirit when oppressed by contact with crafty and hypocritical men" (*The Desire of* Ages, p. 511). It is certain that when Jesus looked at the faces of innocent children He found welcome respite. When He talked and laughed with them, He enjoyed their sincerity and trust. If Christ in person were again to walk on earth, He would again seek the company of children to affirm them and to even be encouraged by them. This is the loving heart of Jesus for children. May His little ones everywhere, whom He created and died for, rejoice that their best and forever Friend sees them as worthy of His regard and encouragement.

When we invite or we get invited to eat and visit, I enjoy conversing with the adults. But I intentionally reach out to each one of the children at the table to ask them questions, listen attentively to their responses, and talk simply and clearly to them. It is not only spiritually beneficial, but it is great fun to listen to their interesting ideas of how they view things around them. It the grace of Christ in the heart that "will lead fathers and mothers to treat their children as intelligent beings, as they themselves would like to be treated" (*The Desire of Ages*, p. 515). Parents often tell me that how much they appreciate my interest in their children, and the real difference it makes. It comes as a surprise to them because they do not usually expect it. You see, children are sometimes treated as a nuisance to be tolerated, or as a burden to be endured. And it is almost like a self-fulfilling prophecy: if we treat them as a bother or an inconvenience, they are more likely to turn out that way; but if we treat them with love, respect, and encouragement, they are apt to do better.

Young and Old to Be Interdependent

By the way, we need to see in our homes, churches, and society at large more examples of reciprocal affirmation between the old and the young. It seems that at the very time the old folks need the young ones, and the young ones need the old folks, is the time when they unfortunately separate from each other. There is no better approach to this dilemma than the Christ-centered, biblical approach: for the young to show respect and a helping hand to the elderly, and for the elderly to show love and wise guidance to the young. For some reason, the young are often kept to themselves, and the elderly as well. It is sad to see what is happening all around us in this regard. It is a regrettable waste of golden opportunities for both generations to mutually benefit from each other's company. You see, the younger generation needs the wisdom of the older generation acquired with age, and the older generation needs the encouragement that their liveliness and optimism brings.

I can testify to the validity of this from my own experience when I was a youngster. And now when I have the chance to take some youngsters with me to visit the elderly in their own homes, nursing homes, or retirement centers I see the affirming smiles and mutual satisfaction in both groups. The most affirming words in this mutual ministry is what Jesus said, that in as much as we do this to the least of these we do it to Jesus Himself (Matt. 25:40). We need to be aware of the so-called Christian books, influenced by today's postmodern philosophy, that advocate independence (rather than interdependence) and separation from the influence of godly parents and family values. This is all done under the artful guise of discouraging parents from stifling the individualism and autonomy of their young people. Some might say that they do not want to encourage codependency, and I totally agree. But here we are encouraging dependence on God and interdependence among each other. Jesus saw that we all (young and old) profoundly impact each others' lives, for He created us to be social beings. We are our brothers' and sisters' keepers, affected by their joys and sorrows.

The Greatness of Childlikeness

Let us go back to see how Jesus related to the little ones that were brought to Him. He is our prime example in affirming children. He loved these little ones, and they knew it and they loved Him in return. They could sense this love emanating from Him, and that is why they were naturally drawn to Him, and longed to be around Him. It seems that He sought opportunities to validate them and make them feel worthwhile. Once the disciples were disputing among themselves as to who would be the greatest in His kingdom. Jesus quickly cautioned them that if that was their attitude, they would never even enter His kingdom, not to say anything about being the greatest.

Christ's Way of Affirmation

Notice the powerful object lesson Jesus used in Mark 9:33–37 to teach His disciples a valuable lesson in the essential virtues of humility and true greatness, and to also encourage a little child as well. Watch Christ's body language and words. He called him, probably by name, indicating His personal interest in him; He set the little child in their midst, signifying the importance of this demonstration; and then He gently held him—enfolding him in His arms, tangibly showing His tender love for him. Then Jesus inseparably connected the acceptance of this child with the acceptance of Him and His Father. There is a perfect union in the Father-Son relationship; and Jesus emphatically placed the receiving of this little one as being on the same lofty level as His oneness with His Father.

Matthew's narrative provides other important exhortations of Christ to the disciples about the indispensable characteristic of becoming childlike, manifesting itself in genuine conversion and true greatness. Jesus asserted: "Assuredly, I say to you, unless you are converted and become as little children, you will by no means enter the kingdom of heaven" (Matt. 18:3). To be childlike does not mean to be childish. And in this example Jesus showed that, in a sense, the little child was more mature in the spiritual matters of His kingdom than His disciples. They showed childishness in their self-centered pettiness and rivalry by setting a goal to be greater than anyone else among them. True greatness is found in a childlike character, manifested in simplicity, innocence, humility, love, trust, and self-forgetfulness. No greater compliment could Jesus have given to this child than to associate his childlike character with spiritual conversion and entrance into His kingdom.

Human Rebuke and Divine Indignation

The disciples had another chance to view children from Christ's perspective. They, being adults, actually rebuked the mothers and tried to separate their children from Jesus. It seems that after Jesus showed such favor to that one child earlier, the word got around, attracting several mothers and their children to Jesus. He affirmed children individually and collectively. The narrative found in Mark 10:13-16 states: "Then they brought young children to Him, that He might touch them; but the disciples rebuked those who brought them. But when Jesus saw it, He was greatly displeased and said to them, 'Let the little children come to Me, and do not forbid them; for of such is the kingdom of God. . . . And He took them up in His arms, put His hands on them, and blessed them.'"

Two strong and opposite emotional reactions on the part of the disciples and Jesus are evident in connection with this narrative. The disciples rebuked the mothers (and by association their children), and Jesus was greatly displeased. Even physically, the disciples wanted to shoo them far away from Him, but to the contrary, Jesus wanted to hold them as close to Him as possible. He touched them, He held them in His arms (to be on the same level), and placed His hands on their heads, and prayed a blessing on them. Such warm and affectionate personal sentiments so vividly displayed are quite amazing, to say the least. It is mentioned only a few times that Christ was indignant about something, and here is one of these times. He actually was very indignant and very displeased with the disciples trying to separate Him from His loved little ones. It was a strong gesture of righteous indignation, and a protective posture in their support.

As if Christ was saying, if you fellows lay a finger on these little kids you are poking the apple of My eye. This protective sentiment toward the children is clothed with a warning or a threat: "But whoever causes one of those little ones who believe in Me to sin, it would be better for him if a millstone were hung around his neck, and he were drowned in the depth of the sea" (Matt. 18:6). No child should ever doubt Jesus' great love and strong affirmation. He is ready to fight for them, warning anyone who would abuse them in any way of capital punishment. Doesn't the Bible say that their angels always behold the Father's face? Yes, handle them with great care for they are close to the heart of the Father, the heart of His Son and the hearts of their guardian angels. That is why we must always extend Christ's hands of love and blessing to them, and show Christlikeness in the way we treat them, so that none of them will stumble, but be drawn to the embrace of their loving Savior.

Heaping Excessive Praise

A note of caution is in order here. We must keep in mind that there is a fine line between flattery and encouragement. Our safety is to simply follow Christ's example in relating to children. Let us not forget that Jesus never flattered children (or anybody for that matter), rather He encouraged and affirmed them. He showed His recognition and appreciation by touching them, holding them close to Him, and blessing them. Children are still a part of this evil world, and they are not yet holy cherubs translated to heaven. Jesus affirmed their childlike love and trust, but did not flatter them in their looks or cute mannerisms.

So in modeling Christ's example as adults—parents, relatives, and teachers—we need to understand the difference between affirming children and heaping unwarranted praise and flattery on them. Nowadays children are sometimes paraded and glorified before others to satisfy the insecurity, pride, and vanity of parents. The end result is neither healthy for the children nor the parents. Some well-meaning parents (and grandparents) incessantly adulate their children as if there are no other children beside theirs in the entire world. What does this do to other parents hearing this? How does this affect the children themselves? "Children need appreciation, sympathy, and encouragement, but care should be taken not to foster in them a love of praise" (*Education*, p. 237).

If we teach and show them that having Jesus as their best Friend, and enjoying His uplifting words cherished in their hearts, then their need of flattery will not have a hold on them. Godly mothers are instructed to "Teach them [their children] that the approbation and smiles of Jesus are of greater value than the praise or flattery or approval of the most wealthy, the most exalted, the most learned of the earth" (*Child Guidance*, p. 41). Of course children have an imperative need—and this need must be met—for sympathy, encouragement, and validation. But we must be careful not to let this evolve into excessive praise and adulation, making them feel as if they are always the center of everything.

By indulging the children in having their own way, parents are fostering self-centeredness and willfulness. Under the guise of helping them to be independent and realizing their self-importance, they grow up to be arrogant, disrespectful, and wanting to be the center of everyone's attention. Fearing to displease their children, parents become overly complimentary to them, and even slavishly follow their foolish whims. Even the highly educated parents and teachers believe that only sweet words and compliments should be used with them. Only the agreeable "yes" should be used, but not the disagreeable "no." Children are supposed to behave in any way they want, but the parents are supposed to restrain themselves from using any disciplinary measures. They are not supposed to firmly stand up to them and assert their God-given leadership prerogatives.

Supposedly all of this misguided love and lax discipline is encouraged in order to help them develop naturally, not stifling their growth and self-worth. These ideas do not come from the Scriptures but from a secular humanistic mindset.

It is true that "The prevailing influence in the world is to suffer the youth to follow the natural turn of their own minds. And if very wild in youth, parents say they will come right after a while, and when sixteen or eighteen years of age, will reason for themselves, and leave off their wrong habits, and become at last useful men and women. What a mistake! For years they permit an enemy to sow the garden of the heart; they suffer wrong principles to grow, and in many cases all the labor afterward bestowed on that soil will avail nothing" (*Testimonies*, vol. 1, p. 403).

In this connection Ellen White follows Christ's example in using a balanced approach in relating to children: love and encourage them, but do not spoil and flatter them. Let us consider carefully the following helpful and cautionary counsel. "The little ones take note of this [indulgence and flattery] and swell with self-importance; they presume to interrupt conversations and become forward and impudent. Flattery and indulgence foster their vanity and willfulness, until the youngest not unfrequently rules the whole family, father and mother included" (*Child Guidance*, p. 140).

"One great reason why so many children are forward, bold, and impertinent is they are noticed and praised too much, and their smart, sharp sayings repeated in their hearing. Endeavor not to censure unduly, nor to overwhelm with praise and flattery. Satan will all too soon sow evil seed in their young hearts, and you should not aid him in his work" (*ibid.*, p. 38). "Their character is built upon sliding sand. Self-denial and self-control have not been molded into their characters. They have been petted and indulged until they are spoiled for practical life. The love of pleasure controls minds, and children are flattered and indulged to their ruin" (*ibid.*, pp. 184, 185).

DISCUSSION QUESTIONS

1. Jesus is a lover of children. What does this fact tell you about His character?

2. Why is it a win-win situation when the older and the younger people maintain a close and reciprocal relationship?

3. What do you think is the difference between childlikeness and childishness? Why is it that we will never enter the kingdom of heaven unless we become childlike?

4. How does godly discipline of our children reveal our genuine and responsible love toward them? Contrast this with misguided or permissive love.

5. Why is excessive praise or the lack of any praise detrimental to our children's spiritual growth and maturity?

CHAPTER THREE

Affirming Friends

*"You are My friends if you do whatever I command you. No longer
do I call you servants, for a servant does not know what his master is
doing; but I have called you friends, for all things that I heard from
My Father I have made known to you"
(John 15:14, 15).*

One of the most profound definitions of friendship is
attributed to the Lebanese writer Khalil Gibran, which I
once read on a greeting card sent to me. He describes a genuine
friend as someone to whom one can pour out all the contents
of one's heart, wheat and chaff together. He keeps what is
worth keeping, and with a gentle breath blows the rest away.
Interestingly, the literal meaning of the writer's name, *Khalil,* is
"friend," which is the same title that is given to Abraham as the
friend of God. "Abraham believed God, and it was accounted
to him for righteousness. And he was called the friend of God"
(Jas. 2:23). This type friendship has to do with love, genuineness,
faithfulness, righteousness, and implicit trust. No wonder James
closely connects this genuine friendship with God to faith and
righteousness.

Friends in Prosperity *and* Adversity

Genuine human friendship is uncommon today. In fact,
many so-called friends reveal, along life's challenging journey,
that they are not the real article. They are there for you in

prosperity; but when adversity threatens, they tend to move on to more pleasant pastures. They are mostly takers not givers, exhausting our time, energy, and resources. They are pleased to let you take the initiative in reaching out to them, but they are hardly intentional in reaching out to you. Pretentious friends can be professional friends, who want to be close to you to get along with you in the workplace, or to use you in advancing their careers. I have had many friends who came to me for counsel and support for many years, and I was more than happy to be there for them. But when I myself was going through a tough time, they simply showed no support in my situation.

Some friends, when they advance in their careers, act as if they never knew you. They act proud and condescending, and the familiar sparkle of a friend that was once there is now gone. These are friends you socialized and ministered with on many occasions, calling them by their first names, laughing and praying with them. A few times in my life I was bold enough to risk asking some of them (I had nothing to lose) what was going on. Were they still the same persons I had known before? The curious thing is that they acted as if everything was as great as before. But, as the saying goes, actions speak louder than words, for you can feel the aloofness whenever you are around them. They act differently, and gradually become distant and detached. However, it is quite telling that when they get demoted, lose their job, retire, or when they need you, then they desire to get close to you again as before, acting as if nothing transpired in the meantime.

Friends, with whom you have associated closely, even for decades, call on you only when they need you to do something for them. Years can pass by before they contact you again; some even drop you for good, just like that. Everything seems to be pleasant as far as you can tell, but all of a sudden they cool off and pull away. If you chance asking them for an explanation, they usually act as if everything is normal, but in reality it is not. That becomes increasingly evident by their continuous coldness, so you move on without ever knowing the truth. We live in a very mobile society, and friends who move away are likely to move away from the friendship which we thought was lasting. This becomes a fulfillment of the saying "Out of sight out of mind." It is not infrequent that I see couples who are dating gradually move on because of moving away.

Why should this be the case? Should not genuine love and friendship remain intact despite circumstances? Genuine friendship is not a role we artfully play or a task we accomplish dictated by circumstances, but a reliable and true mutual relationship among caring human beings. In His friendship with us, Christ affirms His enduring faithfulness and commitment: "And lo, I am with you always, even to the end of the age" (Matt. 28:20). Moreover, He Himself reminds us: "I will never leave you nor forsake you" (Heb. 13:5). This is the kind of friendship we all need, and one which we gratefully can have in Jesus.

Modern society focuses on the task at hand as its priority and consequently depersonalizes who we are as people. It is a sad manifestation of individualism run amuck, which says: I am the center of the world and everyone and everything is here to serve me. But Jesus our example taught and practiced a diametrically opposite philosophy in human relationships: "And whoever desires to be first among you, let him be your slave—just as the Son of Man did not come to be served, but to serve, and to give His life a ransom for many" (Matt. 20:27, 28). God did not make us in His image to simply accomplish a task for Him, but more importantly to fellowship with Him, and to experience a profound sense of being and belonging.

Blood and Spiritual Relations
There are all too many friends who are there for convenience,

expediency, and ulterior motives. That is why being blessed with a genuine friend is a great gift from God that we should greatly appreciate. This serves as a glimpse of Christ as our Friend. And thank God there are a few selfless and genuine friends who reflect Christ in their relationship with us. What the wise man Solomon said in Proverbs 18:24 rings so true, that "there is a friend who sticks closer than a brother." The Hebrew word for friend in this text means someone who loves, hence the likely rendition of a loving friend. This represents Christ's genuine friendship to us actuated by His love. It is altruistic, reliable, unconditional, faithful, and affirming. Friends are likely to change depending on the circumstances, true to the saying "Friends come and friends go."

This type of true friendship is enshrined in the heart of our heavenly Father by making His Son's friends His own friends. "The Father demonstrates His infinite love for Christ, who paid our ransom with His blood, by receiving and welcoming Christ's friends" (*Testimonies*, vol. 6, p. 364). My godly father showed me a glimpse of this dynamic. Because of the love and trust we had for each other, His friends became my friends and my friends became his, for each other's sake. Thus we treated each other's friends as our own.

However, your best Friend Jesus is always loving, reliable, and trustworthy. He is the One who adheres closely to you, even closer than a brother. In the midst of your disappointments and trials, He assures you with His affirming words: "I know your sorrows; I have endured them. I am acquainted with your struggles; I have experienced them. I know your temptations; I have encountered them. I have seen your tears; I also have wept. Your earthly hopes are crushed; but let the eye of faith be uplifted and penetrate the veil, and there anchor your hopes. The everlasting assurance shall be yours that you have a Friend that sticketh closer than a brother" (*Testimonies*, vol. 2, p. 271).

Christ's Way of Affirmation

This Friend Jesus is also our elder Brother, that is why "He is not ashamed to call them brethren" (Heb. 2:11). Here we have the glorious privilege of enjoying both Christ's friendship and brotherhood. Through His sacrifice He became our elder Brother, thus bonding us with the Father and our fellow Christian brothers and sisters with a spiritual bond that is tighter, more authentic, and more enduring than even blood relations. There are many friends who pretend to be friends, but there is the genuine Friend who adheres to us even closer than family. Let us note this relational progression:

1. Pretentious friends for convenience and expediency— no bond as such.

2. Family members such as brothers and sisters—strong blood bonds.

3. Closer even than brothers and sisters—a Friend that "sticks closer than a brother." This is the highest level of relationship that Jesus provides for us. It is a blood and spiritual relationship through His shed blood, His creation, and His continuous fellowship.

This was so clearly demonstrated on the occasion when Christ's mother and brothers came to talk to Him while busily ministering to others. The brothers were the ones who prompted Mary to join them in order to use her to persuade Jesus to modify or restrain His ministry. She was quite likely the unwilling participant, being totally supportive of her Son. Jesus responded: "Who is My mother and who are My brothers? And He stretched out His hand toward His disciples and said, 'Here are My mother and My brothers! For whoever does the will of My Father in heaven is My brother and sister and mother" (Matt. 12:48-50). Yes, Christ had a relationship with His brothers, but it was much stronger with the disciples who were willing to trust and do the will of His Father. This is a spiritual tie which is even stronger than a blood tie, because it is created by the shed blood of Jesus coursing through the lives of His followers, ransomed with His inestimable price.

Friends, How Close?

Even among Christ's friends, there were different levels of closeness, depending on how open their hearts were to His love. Thus in the context of our closeness to our friends and brothers in Christ, this varies depending on the receptivity and willingness to love and do God's will, not our own. Look at Christ's widening circle of friends: John the beloved (1), the inner circle of John, Peter, and James (3), the twelve disciples (12), the seventy He commissioned (70), and the one hundred and twenty He sent forth (120). If Jesus felt the need to have an inner circle, then it is fine for us to need the same as we interact and minister with our brothers, sisters, and friends in Christ.

This does not mean that Christ's disciples were by any means close to being perfect, but were walking with Him in their journey forward. This should give us hope as we walk with Jesus today. Remember the disciples' struggles even to the end. Judas shamefully betrayed Him, Peter cowardly denied Him, Thomas unashamedly doubted Him, and all (except John) impulsively fled for their lives at the urging of Peter. The Lord does not just drop His friends because of their growing pains or shortcomings, but He works with them as long as they are open to Him and willing to cooperate with Him. That is the affirming way He relates to us along life's journey, and that is how we should relate to others.

Reproving and Approving

Take Peter, for instance. Did Jesus affirm him only when he did well? What about when he messed up terribly? There is, for sure, approving affirmation, but is there such a thing as reproving affirmation? Jesus used both approaches with Peter.

He approved of him when he declared through the Father's inspiration that Jesus was indeed the Son of the Living God (Matt. 16:17). But then a few verses later Jesus reproved him when he tried to dissuade Him against His mission to the cross (v. 23). We can also refer to this as exhortative affirmation. It is interesting to note that the same person, Peter, was used by our heavenly Father and by the father of lies, yet Christ patiently worked with His impulsive yet teachable disciple regardless. And He is as willing to work with us today as His friends.

Through His two-edged sword, God cuts the heart in order to mend it. "I wound and I heal," He says in Deuteronomy 32:39. As the Great Physician, Christ has to perform a spiritual operation on us by cutting and repairing where it is needed in order to restore us to spiritual vitality. No one likes surgery, for sure, but there is no healing without cutting, and the One who cuts is the wounded Healer who heals and restores.

It is not attractive for some to think that affirmation may include reproving as well as approving. What Solomon said about reproving affirmation does not resonate with many people in our culture. "Faithful are the wounds of a friend," he states, "but the kisses of an enemy are deceitful" (Prov. 27:6). The Hebrew word "faithful" used here means to be supportive, to be strong, and to be true toward our friends.

Many today, because they are afraid to hurt their friends' feelings, have a weak moral backbone to speak the truth in love and kindness. The loving reproof of a genuine friend may hurt for awhile, but it will heal. Such a friend shows that he is not for sweet empty flattery but for true caring, and is willing to take the risk of being temporarily misunderstood to help his friend. On the other hand, the sweet kisses and empty flattery of enemies may seem pleasant for the moment, but later come back to bite us. On the other hand, responsible love that holds a friend accountable is an authentic expression of altruistic motives that are other-centered not self-centered.

Overflowing with His Love

One of my students was feeling miserable coming to class one day. After class she confided that her boyfriend was hardly kind and complimentary to her at breakfast that morning. "What happened is ruining my day," she said in frustration. Trying to encourage her, I said that her best friend Jesus was very sympathetic and affirming. So even if her boyfriend was not appreciative enough of her, still the King of kings loved her with an everlasting love, showering her with all the kindness and encouragement she needed. It is not the end of the world, so to speak, if someone does not show us enough love and support, because our best Friend Jesus does; and that should make a big difference. Surprised and encouraged at my comments, she said that she had not thought of it that way before.

When a young man and a young woman want to be friends, it is vitally essential that they become close friends with Jesus first. Let Him cover them with His unconditional love and surround them with His stalwart support, then they would see each other from His perspective. And instead of depleting each other of whatever emotions they have, they would be replenished from the real Source. I believe that is the rationale behind what Jesus said about loving Him first and foremost. "He who loves father or mother more than me is not worthy of Me," Jesus instructed His disciples. "And he who loves son or daughter more than Me is not worthy of Me" (Matt. 10:37). It is evident that Jesus wants us to love and honor our parents, cherish our children, and be caring to our friends; but we must love Him more than anyone else. Is this because Christ thinks of Himself first regardless of others? To the contrary, for He knows that the only way we can love our families and friends the best is for Him to fill us with His love as we put Him first. Then such a love for Him and from Him can flow out to others. Without this replenishment from Christ's loving heart, we are indeed self-centered and empty.

Judas Iscariot was also one of the disciples whom Jesus loved, but whenever we think of him we think of the worst of the twelve disciples. After all, he was the one who betrayed and sold His loving Master to the cross for thirty pieces of silver. But even until the bitter end, Jesus loved this thief and traitor. He washed his feet the very night he went out to betray Him. In the condescending act of washing his feet, Jesus was doing His utmost to soften his heart with His love, and to encourage him to repent before he crossed the line of no return. "Jesus alone could read his [Judas'] heart. Yet He did not expose him. Jesus hungered for his soul. . . . The constraining power of that love was felt by Judas. When the Savior's hands were bathing those soiled feet, and wiping them with the towel, the heart of Judas thrilled through and through with the impulse then and there to confess his sin. But he would not humble himself" (*The Desire of Ages*, p. 645).

Wounded in the House of My Friends

Jesus' love was even revealed to this doomed disciple when Judas betrayed Him with a kiss. As the prevailing custom at that time, a kiss on the cheek signified friendship. In response to this kiss of death, Jesus called him a friend. "Friend, why have you come?" (Matt. 26:50). And hearing no response from the traitor, He answered His own question with another question. Calling him by name, Jesus queried: "Judas, are you betraying the Son of Man with a kiss?" (Lk. 22:48). Even those who nailed Him on the cross, He called friends, as recorded in Zechariah 13:6. "And someone will say to him, 'What are these wounds between your arms'? Then He will answer, 'Those with which

I was wounded in the house of my friends.'"

It is quite amazing that Christ refers to those whose hands were besmeared with His blood, "my friends." He also mentions the location of the wounding: their house. The friends' house is supposed to be a place of peace and security, but by their treachery they made it a house of blood. The Redeemer's innocent blood does not cry out in vengeance, but in friendship. The pierced hands are not clenched in defiance, but outstretched to prompt repentance and restoration. Remember also that He prayed for those crucifying Him while He was breathing His last. "Father, forgive them, for they do not know what they do" (Lk. 23:34). This was not simply a polite or a nice act, but serious business to stir their murderous hearts to eventual repentance. Lo and behold! His prayers were actually answered when many of them repented at Peter's Pentecostal preaching.

Genuine friendship with Jesus is never based on our high status or great accomplishments in life, but it is established on our heart-to-heart relationship with Him. All He asks of us, no matter who we are, is to give Him our heart and walk with Him. The Jewish leaders were set against such an idea, and that is why they accused Him of being a "friend of tax collectors and sinners" (Lk. 7:34). These common people were so unlike the Pharisees in that they "heard Him gladly" (Mk. 12:37). That is why they were His friends. The learned and sophisticated closed their ears and sealed their hearts against hearing Him, but the shunned ones opened their hearts and rejoiced at His words of encouragement and hope. This is what constitutes true friendship with Jesus, who came for the purpose of seeking and saving such people.

Loyal Servants and Trusted Friends

So far we have been discussing the blessing of Christ affirming us as His friends and brothers. But what about affirming us as His loyal servants, faithful witnesses, diligent laborers, and dogged followers? Remember what Jesus said in John 15:14, 15 that we are His friends if we do whatever He commands us. This sounds like being His servants, in the sense of being absolutely obedient to Him. Then Jesus continues: "No longer do I call you servants, for a servant does not know what His master is doing; but I have called you friends, for all things that I heard from My Father I have made known to you." The explanation is in the text: a servant in this context is someone who does not know what the master is doing. The disciples are not servants as such (but rather friends) in the sense that they do know the things that their Master heard from the Father. He had taken them into His confidence as loving and trusted friends do, sharing confidential information with them.

The apostle Paul was certainly a solid friend of Jesus, for He took him into His confidence as He entrusted him with many things about the gospel in the region of Arabia. Yet he described himself as His servant in Romans 1:1. "Paul, a servant of Jesus Christ," he writes, "called to be an apostle, separated to the gospel of God." The Greek word for servant is *doulos*, which means "a bond servant," or "a slave." He does not use this word in terms of forced servitude or blind obedience, but in the sense of genuine love, untiring devotion, and total loyalty to his Lord. After all, Jesus purchased Paul and all of us with His precious blood; hence we belong to Him not only by creation but also by redemption. And it is a fact that this kind of "bondage" to Jesus is truly the most liberating from any human bondage in this world.

Therefore, all these terms used to describe our relationship with Jesus convey a certain facet or level of that relationship. But all these descriptions serve to encourage and affirm us in our service to our Master. In summary, here are four such terms:

- *Slave*: Focus on absolute loyalty and obedience to the Master.

- *Servant*: Emphasis on following our Master's example to "serve but not to be served."

- *Brother*: Focus on the reality that through Christ's salvation we are made His brothers and sisters—members of His own family.

- *Friend*: Emphasis on the trust that Jesus feels towards us by taking us into His confidence, and sharing that which devoted friends share with each other.

There are many other instances where Jesus affirmed His disciples and friends. In the Beatitudes, as recorded in Matthew chapter five, Jesus refers to His disciples and other followers listening to His Sermon on the Mount as "blessed." This is a special word that the King of the kingdom of grace uses to wish true happiness for His disciples. Such happiness results from loving the King and following Him. This rich and affirming word, "blessed" can also imply Christ's desire for us to be honored, praised, and highly regarded for bringing honor to Him.

Jesus refers to His disciples as the "salt of the earth," and the "light of the world" (Matt. 5:13, 14). The pronoun "you" in Greek is intentionally emphatic to convey Christ's idea that they themselves indeed are to be the salt and light in this savorless and dark world. It is evident that Christ believes in us and hopes for us in spite of our shortcomings. He encourages us with His affirming words that we can make a profound impact in the world. When we are salted by the savor of His grace, and illumined by the light of His truth, we can be His mighty agents to transform our world for Him.

Jesus affirmed His stressed-out disciples by sympathizing with their predicament of the multiple demands of ministry. I am sure it was an encouragement to them to know that their Master cared deeply about their welfare. He certainly was not a slave master but a merciful master. From early dawn to late night, they labored with Jesus for others. So He compassionately called on them to "Come aside by yourselves and rest a while" (Mk. 6:31). "For there were many coming and going and they did not even have time to eat." In the thick of meeting the endless needs of many hurting people, Jesus plucked His disciples out, so to speak, to provide them with much needed time for rest and recuperation.

Keep Your Courage Up!

It is encouraging to hear from Christ's lips that we are very valuable to God. His care for us is so great that we do not have to worry or be anxious. And when we seek Him first, he provides for all our needs. "Look at the birds of the air, for they neither sow nor reap nor gather into barns; yet your heavenly Father feeds them. Are you not of more value than they?" (Matt. 6:26). Also Jesus goes on to assure us of how much He values and cares for us. "But the very hairs on your head are all numbered. Do not fear therefore; you are of more value than many sparrows." (Matt. 10:30, 31). The idea here is this: If God cares so much for even birds, how exceedingly more He does care for His special human creatures created in His image and redeemed by Christ's blood. If God notices when even a simple sparrow hurts, how much more He does hurt when we hurt. Finally, His meticulous care is so great that He even counts the hair on our heads! We all care about the hair of our heads, for sure, but how many care enough to count every single hair? God does!

Jesus employed the most positive words to encourage His fearful disciples. He would often say to them to be cheerful, to be of good courage, and not be afraid. At one time, for instance, they were tossed back and forth by angry sea waves and howling winds. Greatly frightened that a ghost was walking by on the water, but instead it was Jesus. "Be of good cheer! It is I; do not be afraid" (Matt. 14:27). One cannot help but be touched by Christ's love and care for His disciples. A heart full with encouragement when it is needed most. He comes across as a true Friend who assures you in your trouble, and lifts up your sagging morale by telling you that He is there for you, not to worry, cheer up, and that He will take care of you. Thank God for such an awesome Friend in times of need!

When we are vexed by the storms of life, He declares to us, "Peace, be still!" (Mk. 4:39). When we are afflicted with the troubles of this evil world, He assures us to be full of courage. "These things I have spoken to you, that in Me you may have peace. In the world you will have tribulation; but be of good cheer, I have overcome the world" (Jn. 16:33). To be of good cheer in the original Greek means more precisely to be of good courage, or full of courage. If Christ were to use our jargon today, He would say, "Keep your courage up!" This affirming speech to be courageous is even more appreciated when contrasted with the tribulations we have in this world. But happily Christ was victorious over this world; hence we may receive His peace that passes all understanding. In His encouraging words, He deals with the troubling realities of this wicked world, but He also provides the overwhelming remedy of His presence, courage, and peace.

Well Done!

Then there are two great statements of affirmation in Matthew 25 in connection with the parable of the talents, and the final judgment. The faithful servant is told by his lord: "Well done, good and faithful servant; you were faithful over a few things, I will make you ruler over many things. Enter into the joy of your lord" (Matt. 25:21). Then Christ presents the criteria for the final judgment: the way we treat the least of those around us is exactly the way we treat Jesus Himself. The righteous ones seem unaware that they were doing anything special for Jesus. They do not flatter themselves of how good they are, contrary to the lost ones who do. They are humble and self-effacing. Yet the encouraging recognition Jesus bestows on them is priceless, for they are kind, caring, and compassionate to Jesus. The King will compliment them saying: "Assuredly I say to you, in as much as you did it to one of the least of these my brethren, you did it to Me" (Matt. 25:40).

On another occasion Jesus assures His faithful disciples of their rich reward for leaving everything and following Him. Peter asks Him: "See, we have left all and followed You. Therefore what shall we have?" (Matt. 19:27). Look at the great hope He engenders in them, and the affirming way Jesus answers Peter and the disciples in verses 28-30.

1. They will sit on twelve thrones to judge the twelve tribes of Israel.

2. In leaving material possessions and dear family members for His sake, they will receive a hundredfold in return.

3. Then at His coming they will inherit eternal life.

4. Furthermore, Jesus reiterates His hope and regard for His devoted disciples, when at the end He will reward them with the glories of heaven. "Then the righteous will shine forth as the sun in the kingdom of their Father" (Matt. 13:43). This is not any ordinary light that shines, but a brilliant light bursting through the dismal darkness of a doomed world. That is how Jesus feels about our glorious potential through Him as the Light of the universe. In a descriptive sense, He compares us to the dazzling blast of the sun's light erupting through thick clouds of darkness.

How is it possible for us who are darkness to ever become that light? Paul provides the answer in that we become light in His light: "For once you were darkness," he states, "but now you are light in the Lord. Walk as children of light" (Eph. 5:8). Paul also explains that God "has delivered us from the power of darkness and translated [transferred] us into the kingdom of the Son of His love" (Col. 1:13). Jesus must really believe in us against all odds to call us "out of darkness into His marvelous light" (1 Pet. 2:9). To Christ we are a bright light to shine forth as the blazing sun. How more affirming can He be than that!

DISCUSSION QUESTIONS

1. What is your definition of a genuine friend? Why is that so?

2. What is the significance of having Jesus as our "Friend" and "Brother"? How are we related to Him by blood and by spirit? What difference does this wonderful affirmation make in our lives when taken to heart?

3. How do you distinguish between approving affirmation and exhortative affirmation? Why are both types of affirmation essential and beneficial for the nurture of genuine friendship?

4. How do you explain it when Jesus referred to Judas as His "friend" upon betraying Him with a kiss? How do you compare this with His reply to the question: "What are these wounds in your hands"?

5. What does it mean to be a servant or a friend of Jesus? Is there a difference? Compare and contrast.

CHAPTER FOUR

Escaping Foolish Flattery

*"They speak idly everyone with his neighbor; with flattering lips and
a double heart they speak" (Psalm 12:2).*
*"A lying tongue hates those who are crushed by it, and a flattering
mouth works ruin" (Proverbs 26:28).*

"Flattery won't do you any good." This is what we
sometimes hear as a retort to any expression of genuine
compliment or false flattery. Some have decided to avoid any
form of affirmation—giving it or receiving it—in order not to
succumb to flattery. It is a wary approach of letting go of the
good in order to avoid the bad. The expression of throwing the
baby out with the bath water is quite apt in this regard. Taking
the expression, "Flattery won't do you any good," for its face value
is quite correct. Solomon says that "a flattering mouth works
ruin." There is a misconception as to what constitutes altruistic
affirmation and abject adulation. Some respond to any form
of compliment as flattery to be shunned; others covet outright
flattery to assuage their insecurities. It is evident that there is
a gaping hole in the human heart for genuine affirmation. Yet
because of all the misuse and misconception of this vital subject,
it becomes a hindrance rather than a helpful tool for human
communication. As we shall see, the Bible is always on the side
of genuine affirmation and never on the side of foolish flattery.

Escaping Foolish Flattery

Validation Not Vanity

It is unfortunate that the very thing that people desperately need and long for is the exact thing they misunderstand, confuse, and needlessly avoid. They confuse validation with vanity. And to properly clarify this important issue, we must follow Christ's example in seeing others from His perspective. Thus it is essential for them to understand that to validate others is to recognize, support and uphold them in Christ. Another verb that is a close cousin to validate is to value: to make others feel that they are valuable and valued for whom they are in the body of Christ. Vanity is vastly different than value, for vanity is worthless and value is worth something. Vanity implies futility, and value implies fruitfulness. From Christ's perspective, our ultimate value is indeed worth His life sacrificed on the cross. Vanity is never a part of God's plan for our lives, for it is vacuous, vain, self-conceited, and self-flattering.

Whenever these two opposite spheres—altruistic affirmation and abject adulation—are misunderstood and misapplied, the effect is detrimental for everyone involved. If you sincerely validate someone for performing a task well, for the purpose of encouraging him, and he responds that what he did was nothing, then he is likely taking it as a flattering comment—the opposite of what you had intended. The end result is that you feel like you were misunderstood, and wished that you had not said what you said. The recipient of a genuine compliment in such a situation deprives himself of the well-meaning support of others. What can be a win-win interaction is reduced to a lose-lose proposition. Both parties can win if the genuine compliment is taken as intended. Both, the affirmer and the affirmed, can be mutually appreciated and encouraged.

Authenticity Not Ambiguity

There is also ambivalence as to what constitutes public

adulation and private affirmation. In our society today there is sometimes excessive public flattery and impressive commendation as seen, for example, in the introduction of public speakers and performers. But unfortunately there is only meager private, one-to-one affirmation. A public speaker is introduced with great fanfare about his awesome speaking skills; and although he does a great job, he is usually not affirmed in what he has just presented by the very person who introduced him—though he sees him face-to-face right after the presentation.

There seems to be a disconnect between a public and a private response. If we truly believe and experience what we say about the speaker, then why don't we say something encouraging to him right after? If we are afraid we may puff him up privately, why then do we puff him up publicly? Genuine commendations are often received second hand. Frequently parents tell me how much their kids appreciate my teaching, yet I often do not hear directly from the students themselves. No doubt there is a reluctance to seem to ingratiate themselves toward their professor, yet isn't there room for personal and genuine affirming words, especially if praise is given to God?

I have also observed this unfortunate kind of flattery when someone compliments a colleague directly with wonderful words, but then acts just the opposite when away from him. We seem to be programmed to be nice in someone's face, but ugly behind his back. We seem to have refined the art of giving the impression that we like someone and what he does, but our heart is far away from this pretension. Before a committee is convened, I sometimes hear a member strongly supporting another member's idea, only for that member to say nothing during the committee deliberations. Flattery in this connection has to do with a conflicted person whose outward behavior contradicts his inner conviction. Thankfully, with Jesus He means what He says and He says what He means. There is no incongruity between His words and His heart.

Let me relate an incident with a car mechanic who did a great job on my car. After paying him for his work, I sincerely thanked him for a job well-done. He paid no attention to what I said as he continued working on another car. I thought that he possibly did not hear me, so I repeated what I said. Puzzled and a little irritated, he looked at me and said: "This is my job. You paid me for it, didn't you?" Leaving his garage, I thought to myself, isn't there more to life than doing a job and getting paid for it? Yes there is. Why deprive ourselves of the joy and blessing of mutual encouragement and appreciation as we interact with each other? We are so focused on the task at hand that we do not seem to care how people are affected by our actions. At the end of the day this is what brings meaning and satisfaction to one's life. Work and money will end someday, but kindness and consideration will last a lifetime.

As a university professor, I have the chance to interact with many students at different levels of their experience. It is always interesting to observe their social interaction in terms of dating and courtship. I frequently hear such comments: "You guys look so great together!" A friend impulsively wishes to please this young couple hanging out together. "You two make such a great couple." Another acquaintance hastily blurts out, intending to curry favor with them. Sadly, a month later, this highly complimented couple brake up the relationship for good. Quite a few of the same complimentary friends suddenly evolve into incriminating friends, saying that they had always thought there was something wrong with the relationship. That the breakup did not come as a surprise to them, for they had the feeling that it was not going to work out. Now they say it!

How would we describe the behavior of these friends? Perhaps they mean no harm by their comments; they just want to be nice. Do they realize that they have unduly encouraged the couple to be more serious, especially when knowing there is something wrong with the relationship to begin with? Is this outright flattery and insincere praise? Are these flattering compliments meant to ingratiate themselves to the couple? It is evident that flattery occurs when a host heaves praise with his tongue in introducing a guest, but in his heart does not believe a thing he has just said. I guess that he merely wants to come across polite and complimentary, probably because that is what is expected of him.

Self-Adulation and Self-Marketing

We live in a society where many people crave too much attention, and strive to market themselves by impressing others. All such self-promotion is enhanced by the electronic media such as in Facebook, MySpace, Twitter, and Skype. This is a most sophisticated high-tech way of self-adulation. There is such a huge misconception and confusion about this topic that the average person does not know how to properly relate to it. People are not sure how to carefully navigate the difference between compliment and flattery, affirmation and adulation. Add to this the difficulty of discerning others' motives in their interaction with each other. Are these motives altruistic or ulterior? Are these overtures for your benefit or their benefit, or for reciprocal benefits—a mutual admiration society?

Webster's Dictionary defines flattery as an "excessive, untrue, or insincere praise; exaggerated compliment or attention; blandishment." Flattery has to do with insincerity and wrong motive. Insincerity: because the praise is unwarranted, untrue, and too excessive. Wrong motive: because the excessive compliment is used to ingratiate one's self or to please others in order to gain favor for one's own advantage. No doubt you have witnessed an individual sweet-talking someone on how he is the best in every way, using superlatives along the way. "You are the best, you are the most talented," and so on. Be careful whenever you hear such exaggerated overtures.

I have witnessed this firsthand in my ministry and in others' as well. It can be described as a love-hate relationship: they build you up as the greatest in every way, as someone incapable of making any mistakes. They seem to set you up with excessive praise, without even knowing you that much, in order to use you for their covert or overt agenda. Then they often turn on you if you do not respond to them the way they want you to. What causes people to become flatterers? Here are some possible reasons for our consideration:

- Need for security. They need to flatter others in the hope that they will be liked by them.

- Need for control. They think that if they massage others' egos, they can sway them to their side to exercise control over them to do their bidding.

- Need to be loved. They imagine that if they heave deceptive compliments on others, such will be attracted to them and love them.

- Need to please. They are people-pleasers. They cannot handle confrontation or conflict, so they try hard to please others by being "yes" people, who practically agree to anything, so that they will not be rejected.

Self-Flattery

When we think of flattery we frequently think of people flattering or being flattered. But it is becoming more fashionable in our time to be engaged in self-adulation under the guise of enhancing one's self-esteem. It was the boxer Muhammad Ali who gloated: "I am the greatest." And Nebuchadnezzar reached the zenith of self-flattery when he boasted: "Is not this great

Babylon that I have built for a royal dwelling by my mighty power and for the honor of my majesty?" (Dan. 4:30). This Babylonian king was the epitome of what Solomon wrote: "Pride goes before destruction and a haughty spirit before a fall" (Prov. 16:18).

Politicians tell us unashamedly how much better they are than all other politicians. They seem willing to do anything to please and flatter the electorate in order to get their votes; yet when the elections are over, things tend to go back to normal. One of my students was failing in all of his classes a week before the final exams. Concerned about his dismal status, I asked if I could help him to do better. He brushed my helpful gesture aside and said that he was much better academically than I thought. As an optimistic person (but unrealistic), he did not want me to worry about him because he had it in him to handle it just fine, and to turn things around. Unfortunately his self-conceit led to his self-delusion, resulting in failure for the whole semester.

Biblical View of Self-Flattery

The Bible talks about those who foolishly flatter themselves. The wicked man "flatters himself in his own eyes, when he finds out his iniquity," because he tries to gloss over his evil by heaping compliments upon himself. He presumptuously hopes to convince himself that he is alright when he is not. It is foolish to assume that we can, no matter how hard we try, flatter ourselves out of our known iniquities. (See Ps. 36:2).

This reminds us of the rebellious person in Deuteronomy 29:19 when he chooses to walk according to his own inclinations and be out of harmony with God's will. God appeals to His people to choose blessing and life not cursing and death. Well, that person knows that God cannot bless him in his rebelliousness, so he actually blesses himself. He is trying to explain away the dire consequence of his waywardness by burying it with self-adulation. Here is the text: "And so it may not happen, when he hears the words of this curse, that he blesses himself in his heart, saying, 'I shall have peace, even though I walk in the imagination of my heart'—as if though the drunkard could be included with the sober." We cannot arrogantly pretend that we can bless ourselves, for God is the only One who has that unique prerogative to bless us.

Christ's example of humility stands in clear contrast to the above example of self-conceit. In His response to the Jews' vicious attacks, He humbly asserts: "If I honor Myself, My honor is nothing. It is My Father who honors Me . . ." (Jn. 8:54). Although Christ had every right to honor Himself, He waited for His Father to honor Him. In His testimony here Jesus fulfilled the wise counsel of Proverbs 27:2. "Let another man praise you, and not your own mouth; a stranger, and not your own lips." This reminds me of the time when I gave a public speaker a sincere compliment for his good presentation. Imagine, he took me aside and eagerly unloaded on me all the other great points in his performance, as though my simple compliment was not enough for him. Apparently he wanted to make sure that I was aware of all the wonderful things about his speaking talents that I might have missed.

Self-flattery never leads to Christlikeness in one's life. It never brings about real satisfaction, for it simply heightens one's insecurity and the insatiable need to impress others. Genuine blessing and honor come only from Christ, and others who are like Christ in character.

The prideful display of the praying Pharisee in the temple is another form of self-flattery. In Luke 18:9-14 the narrative of this parable reveals the heart of a man full of self-centeredness, self-conceitedness, self-trust, and self-justification. He comes across as one telling God how fortunate He is to have such a wonderful person as himself coming before Him. Among all the despicable people coming to pray, finally God must feel so blessed to have one righteous person come around for a change. He reminds God of that (in case the Omniscient forgot!) by effusively heaping praise upon himself as if saying, "I am much better than others in every way, I even fast twice a week, I tithe everything I have, and in conclusion I am sure by now You are quite impressed."

Risking to Deceive Self and Daring to Flatter God

Words can be deceiving, as the saying goes, especially flattering words about ourselves. Eventually we may come to believe them as true. Many are thus deceived, as the praying Pharisee, in highlighting their accomplishments before others. Often such persons do not feel appreciated enough, so they are driven to remind others of their wonderful qualities in case they had been forgotten. It is a fact, isn't it, that the more we crave men's applause the less we experience God's approval. Jesus makes this issue clear in connection with the judgment. "Many will say to Me in that day, 'Lord, Lord, have we not prophesied in Your name, cast out demons in Your name, and done many wonders in Your name.'" Then Jesus pronounces the verdict against them: "And then I will declare to them, 'I never knew you; depart from Me, you who practice lawlessness'" (Matt. 7:22, 23).

Those who flatter themselves represent pretentious Christians who utter the correct words, but do not live the life of Christ. Their self-conceit leads them to question the awareness and fairness of the Judge of the whole earth. They showcase before Him their most impressive deeds: prophesying, exorcism, and working miracles. There are supernatural manifestations inspired by the evil one that have nothing to do with true godliness. Many are drawn to the easy religion of substituting some spectacular spiritual experience for loving God with all the heart and doing His will. The most remarkable miracle is a transformed life wrought by the indwelling Spirit of God. Christ is never impressed by an exciting spiritual performance, but by our unreserved commitment to know Him and to be transformed by Him.

Being self-conceited before the all-knowing God is a deadly delusion, and the worst sort of self-flattery. If some are audacious enough to parade such self-imposed illusion before God, then they can more readily congratulate themselves before their fellow human beings. "Nevertheless they flattered Him with their mouth, and they lied to Him with their tongue" (Ps. 78:36). How more arrogant can a person be than to flatter God! This is so different than the genuine praise to God from a converted heart. This is flagrant hypocrisy as Jesus described it: "These people draw to Me with their mouth, and honor Me with their lips, but their heart is far from Me" (Matt. 15:8). So tragic: close with their mouth, but far away with their heart. Honoring God is not merely something we talk, but mostly something we walk.

This flattery of God has also to do with uselessly trying to please Him in order to manipulate Him to gain a certain advantage. That is the sorry condition of God's people described in Ezekiel 33:31. They pretend to be loving, close, and obedient to God, but they do not do His will. "For with their mouth they show much love, but their hearts pursue their own gain." Their rebellion of the heart is so subtle and deceptive that they can fill their mouths with many loving words for the sole advantage of getting their way. God is not mocked for He knows well the heart, and discerns our innermost motives. Because God deals only with truth and authenticity, He hates it when we try to please Him with our false words, and cannot endure our pretentious spiritual display.

People-Pleasers

Flattery manifests itself also in being people-pleasers, attempting to quench the thirst for personal acceptance and security. This kind of pleasing flattery is not necessarily intended to hurt others, but is born out of a desperate need to be loved, approved, and applauded. Such "yes" persons are so driven to please that they say whatever is agreeable at the moment. They also tend to avoid accountability, conflict, and confrontation at any cost, fearing that meeting such challenges may result in disagreement and disapproval. They do not seem to know that their insatiable need for love and approval can only be satisfied by God; instead they look for that in all the wrong places.

People pleasers are desperate to enjoy immediate satisfaction that they overlook the long-range consequences of their actions. To them pleasing their fellowmen men overcomes pleasing their Maker, and hunger for human applause overwhelms their real need for divine approval. In the long run it does not really matter how many friends are pleased with us, or how much they approve of us. Such experience is shallow, temporary, and costly. What will matter the most when Jesus returns? Pleasing Him or pleasing others? Will not His divine approval dwarf our human applause? He is not going to ask us if we are liked or are popular, but rather if we truly know Him.

Jeremiah aptly describes the untenable human condition of seeking the emptiness of human applause rather than the fullness of divine approval. God says that His people "have committed two evils: they have forsaken Me, the fountain of living waters, and hewn themselves cisterns—broken cisterns that can hold no water" (Jer. 2:13). It is about meeting their own needs rather than letting God meet their needs. It is discarding the real source of their help, and embracing an illusory substitute. He is the source of the living and ever flowing waters they desperately need. Why would they ever substitute the fake stuff of leaky cisterns for the genuine article of flowing springs? In the Middle East where I was born, a flowing refreshing spring is of inestimable value to anyone fortunate enough to have it on his property. In that region where water is very precious, it would the height of foolishness to discard such an immeasurable blessing for a leaky cistern that does not even keep its stagnant water.

Jesus says that He is the living water, and He invites us to drink deeply and be satisfied. And when our thirst for acceptance and security is quenched by this living water, then it can flow from us unto others. "If anyone thirsts, let him come to Me and drink. He who believes in Me, as the Scripture has said, out of his heart will flow rivers of living water" (Jn. 7:37, 38). Jesus desires that we not only drink from His River of life, but become unstoppable rivers of living water ourselves, overflowing with His abundant supply. What great affirmation especially for the ones who feel their lack and deprivation! By God's grace, the quenched become the quenchers, and the supplied become the suppliers.

Divine Approval Not Human Applause

The apostle Paul had a lot to say about people-pleasing and self-commending. He deliberately made the pertinent point that people-pleasing was never a part of his approach to ministry. Instead of focusing on pleasing people, he focused on pleasing God. He was following in the footsteps of Jesus when He said: "The Father has not left Me alone, for I always do those things that please Him" (Jn. 8:29). The key for Paul in this area of commendation is first and foremost God's approval. And in that strong position of pleasing God from our heart, we effectually dispense with flattery and people-pleasing.

He tells the Thessalonian believers: "as we have been approved by God to be entrusted with the gospel, even so we speak, not as pleasing men, but God who tests our hearts. For neither at any time did we use flattering words . . ." (1 Thess. 2:4, 5). Let us note the progression in Paul's thinking as seen in this passage:

- The approval of God is of supreme importance in our ministry and relationships.

- The trust of God is crucial and affirming in sharing the good news with others.

- God's approval gives no allowance for deceit, but only truth spoken with a clear conscience.

- God's approval leads to pleasing God, but never tolerates a ministry for the purpose of pleasing men.

- God's approval tolerates no flattering words cloaked in conceit and covetousness.

- God's approval rejects self-centeredness that makes greedy demands on others.

- God's approval does not lead us to seek glory from others—neither within nor without the church—but to render all honor and glory to Him. "For he who glories, let him glory in the Lord" (1 Cor. 1:31).

Then Paul developed this thought further: "For not he who commends himself is approved, but whom the Lord commends" (2 Cor. 10:18). The emphasis should always be on divine approval of anything good we do and not on human approval, certainly not self-approval. There is no room here for human boastfulness, for whatever success we experience must be attributed to God the source of all blessings. He gives power to think and to work. For "in Him we live and move and have our being" (Acts 17:28). Our appropriate response to even genuine affirmation must always give credit to God. "Praise to

God," "To God be the glory," "It is only by His grace," "Without Him we can do nothing." Such responses recognize and show appreciation of the blessings bestowed, yet they give the credit and glory to God.

The hypocrites in Christ's time went as far as using spiritual activities such as charitable giving, praying, and fasting to attract attention to themselves. They sought human applause, not divine approval, and they received the reward they looked for. (See Matt. 6:1-18). Paul, a former Pharisee, recognized the priority of pleasing God first and foremost when he wrote: "For do I now persuade men, or God? Or do I seek to please men? For if I still pleased men, I would not be a servant of Christ" (Gal. 1:10). To be a faithful servant of Christ is to be engaged in the sacred enterprise of saving souls, not pleasing people.

Accountability Rather Than Accommodation

If this is indeed our priority, then we are liberated from the bondage of impressing people into the freedom of serving our Master. Striving to lead the erring ones to Jesus to be saved may stir up their passions to resist God's appeals. It may be unpleasant for them to clearly see their errors and sinful ways. They may struggle when the appeal is made to truly repent and humbly follow Christ. But the business of Christ's faithful followers is to save rather than to please, to be faithful rather than to be fashionable. Pleasing the erring is taking the easy and irresponsible way out.

Accommodation takes the place of accountability, compromise is substituted for commitment, and so-called tolerance is traded for temperance. There are many negative consequences for becoming caught up in pleasing others and not honoring God. It is a fact that you can never please people enough, and if you think so, then you enable them to stagnate, and carry on as usual. Consequently, in the process you waste so much energy that you become impotent to save the lost. To be free of the worry to please others gives you the courage and energy to do what is right before God.

Under the guise of sympathizing with others in their waywardness, we sometimes extend to them mistaken kindness and false compliments. We may think we are helping them, but to the contrary, we are hurting them. Under the façade of misguided love, we shower the rebellious with injurious flattery and phony praise. In order to please the erring, we sacrifice upholding the right principles. "There is nothing which will please the people better than to be praised and flattered when they are in darkness and wrong, and deserve reproof" (*Testimonies,* vol. 3, p. 345). Being flattered makes us feel good when we are in the wrong. This helps to appease our guilty conscience, and gloss over our need to humble ourselves in repentance. Such are the kisses of an enemy that return to bite us with ruin. "You should be guarded against flattery. Whoever is foolish enough to flatter you cannot be your true friend. Your true friends will caution, entreat, and warn you, and reprove your faults" (*ibid.,* p. 226).

You have heard of the reference to the so-called "mutual admiration society." This implies that friends enjoy the shallow practice of mutually showering each other with flattery. Many know this expression of praise to be contrived, but they still like it anyway because it serves as an intoxicant to give them a temporary reprieve from reality. Such a careless practice will prove injurious because it challenges no one to deal with the real issues of life. It is like what Jesus said about the blind leading the blind; they both fall into a pit of mutual loss. "He [wayward youth] is not to be lifted up by the aid of flattery. No one is authorized to deal out to the soul this *delusive intoxicant of Satan*" (*Fundamentals of Christian Education,* p. 305, emphasis supplied).

Let us beware that Satan employs fatal flattery as a most subtle allurement to inevitable demise.

"We need to shun everything that would encourage pride and self-sufficiency; therefore we should beware of giving or receiving flattery or praise. It is Satan's work to flatter. He deals with flattery as well as in accusing and condemnation. Thus he seeks to work the ruin of the soul" (*Christ's Object Lessons*, p. 161). Satan, being the father of lies, skillfully employs any tool at his disposal to undermine God's plan for us. God uses a loving, balanced, and realistic approach in helping to lift us up to higher ground. He encourages where it is warranted, and He reproves where it is necessary. He lovingly deals with us where we are, but He does not leave us there. Satan employs extreme tactics: he either drives sinners to the ground in despair, or he flatters them to the hilt. Either way he wins.

Christ's Way Is Still the Way

Christ never used flattery with anyone as a means of taking advantage of or of eliciting a response or commitment. He used altruistic affirmation, gracious persuasion, loving exhortation, and stirring curiosity to draw others to Himself. "Jesus never flattered men. He never spoke that which would exalt their fancies and imaginations" (*The Desire of Ages*, p. 254). But He often affirmed the faith in God of those whom He healed. In so doing, He recognized both the power of His Father to heal, and the trusting faith of the healed to grasp that divine power. "Flattery is a part of the world's policy, but it is no part of Christ's policy" (*Fundamentals of Christian Education*, p. 304). One of the best comments on Christ's non–flattering but encouraging approach is found on page 80 of the book *Education*. "In every human being He discerned infinite possibilities. He saw men as they might be, transformed by His grace. . . . Looking upon them with hope, He inspired hope. Meeting them with confidence,

He inspired trust. Revealing in Himself man's true ideal, He awakened, for its attainment, both desire and faith."

Christ's simple and straight-forward approach in relating to others must become the example we follow. He clearly and succinctly said: "But let your 'Yes' be 'Yes,' and your 'No' be 'No.' For whatever is more than these is from the evil one" (Matt. 5:37). The power of this injunction lies in its unwavering and unpretentious candor and clarity. Like a two-edged sword, it cuts through the maze of conceit and deceit, and pierces to the depths of inner motives. This declaration of Jesus causes the offender to be offended, and the deceiver to be defensive. All sorts of excuses are given as to why the truth may be shaded. Taking a defensive stance, they justify their veiled dishonesty by appealing to practicality and expediency.

Look at the world of politics and business, for example. After awhile one gets tired and mystified at all the empty promises and equivocal answers. It is becoming harder to get straight answers from people. You strive to peel layer after layer to hopefully get to the kernel of truth. To all such Christ unequivocally takes a firm and clear stand for truthfulness in all walks of life. "For whatever is more than these," Jesus asserts, "is from the evil one." The demonstrative pronoun "these" refers back to the antecedent's two simple words of "yes," and "no." Whatsoever goes beyond these two unassuming declarations is from the arch deceiver. No matter how shrewdly we try to get around this we simply cannot, because Jesus said if we do we are inspired by the evil one. It is so simple, isn't it? No "if" and "but" about it.

Christ's words recorded in Matthew 5:37 "Condemn the deceptive compliments, the evasion of truth, the flattering phrases ... *Everything* that Christians do should be as transparent as the sunlight. Truth is of God; deception, in *every one of its myriad forms*, is of Satan; and whoever in anyway departs from the straight line of truth is betraying himself into the power of the wicked one" (*Mount of Blessing*, p. 68, emphasis supplied). In emulating Christ's example in being truthful, we need to be directed by Him who is the truth embodied. We need Him to transform our inner motives and cleanse our hidden thoughts, because telling the truth goes beyond mere words. "How often pride, passion, personal resentment, color the impression given. A glance, a word, even an intonation of the voice, may be vital with falsehood. Even facts may be stated as to convey a false impression" (*ibid.*).

Jesus was all for prayer, fasting, and alms-giving, for sure; but the pretentious way the Pharisees went about this was abhorrent to Him. These spiritual activities were intended to draw the participants closer to God, and thus to bring glory and honor to Him. However, the religious leaders of Christ's day were fastidious practitioners of religious activities in order to elicit flattery and commendation from others. (See Matthew 6:1-18). What really counts is the motive of the heart. Is it purified by the humble spirit of Christ, or is it polluted by the conceited spirit of man? "Jesus rebuked their ostentation, declaring that God does not recognize such service and that the *flattery and admiration* of the people, which they so eagerly sought, was the only reward they would ever receive. . . . Those who desire words of *praise and flattery*, and feed upon them as a sweet morsel, are Christians *in name only*" (*ibid.*, p. 80, emphasis supplied).

Jesus longed for His disciples to reveal before the world the light of His truth, the savor of His character, and the fragrance of His life. But in the process of revealing Him we become changed into His likeness. It is like what John the Baptist testified when he beheld Jesus: "He must increase and I must decrease" (Jn. 3:30). He becomes so prominent in our lives that He squeezes self out. He appears and self disappears, so the glory and honor may go to Him only. "Let your light so shine before men, that they may see your good works and glorify your Father in heaven" (Matt. 5:16). What did Jesus mean by this? What role does God play, and what role do we play in terms of recognition and praise?

First, Jesus affirms His disciples as light bearers for Him, and for their good works. Others are not to be dazzled by the light but are able to be attracted to what the light reveals around it.

Second, people are not to flatter the light bearers, but to praise Jesus the light of the world. We simply reflect His light by the "good works" He reveals through us.

Third, others are not to adulate us for such good works, but they are to glorify our heavenly Father who is the power behind these worthy works.

Fourth, Jesus' encouraging affirmation is bestowed upon us for our willingness to become light bearers, and the praise, honor, and glory go to the Source of all the life and light. It is alright for the light's rays to show our good works as long as this points others heavenward.

"By their good works Christ's followers are to bring glory, not to themselves, but to Him through whose grace and power they are wrought. It is through the Holy Spirit that every good work is accomplished, and the Spirit is given to glorify, not the receiver, but the Giver" (*Mount of Blessing*, p. 80).

In conclusion, we want to look at Jude's counsel to the believers in the light of their Lord's return. He boldly sounds the warning about false teachers who in the last days will "mouth great swelling words, flattering people to gain advantage" (Jude 16). This counsel to watch out for flatterers is particularly pertinent to our times. Indeed it is set in the eschatological context of Christ's glorious coming. Jude appeals to Enoch's ancient prophecy concerning the judgment of the ungodly. Mouthing great swelling words of flattery for their own selfish desires, is looked upon with great divine disapproval and condemnation. That is why it must be incumbent upon us to heed this warning against the superficiality, partiality, and egocentricity of flatterers as we prepare to meet Jesus. Like Enoch of old, let us faithfully walk with our Lord in truth and righteousness, so that when He returns we will be prepared to meet Him.

DISCUSSION QUESTIONS

1. How can you tell when someone is flattering you or affirming you?

2. Why do some people have the propensity to flatter others around them? What are some of the reasons behind the insatiable need to be people-pleasers?

3. What does the Bible say about self-flattery? How does that become a hindrance to one's spiritual maturity?

4. What is the difference between praising God and flattering God? What does the latter reveal about one's true spiritual condition? What is the only true remedy for this condition?

5. Why is it in our human nature that leads us to crave human applause rather than divine approval? How can divine approval become of supreme importance to us?

CHAPTER FIVE

Affirming Women

*"And Jesus said to her, 'Neither do I condemn
you; go and sin no more'" (John 8:11).
"But Jesus said, 'Let her alone. Why do you trouble her?
She has done a good work for Me'" (Mark 14:6).*

Once I conducted a week of spiritual emphasis at a
Christian high school. In addition to giving my public
presentations, I also visited many of the students and faculty
members. Dropping by one of the teachers in her office, I
discovered that she had taught English for almost a quarter
century. I shared an encouraging Bible promise and prayed with
her. As I was leaving I tried to affirm her by saying that I was
thankful to God for a committed Christian teacher like her who
taught English writing to restless teenagers for so many years. To
me that was quite an accomplishment! Her eyes became moist
as she confided that no one had ever expressed any gratitude
for her long service. The times when she was contacted were
often about some complaint or criticism. She never felt that
she had done enough or had ever been truly appreciated. Her
superiors had had countless chances to speak with her, yet none
had ever seized the opportunity to say something encouraging
or supportive.

An administrative secretary once told me that she had
worked for her institution's administrator for many years
without her ever knowing how he felt about her work. She
had doubled her efforts as she faithfully accomplished what he

wanted. Never once did he recognize or compliment her good work. Thankfully Jesus is not that way. He often let people with whom He interacted, know how He felt about them by an affirming word or by loving exhortation. In this chapter we will study some examples of how Jesus related to women. His approach to them was radical, in many ways, especially in His respect and validation of them.

The Mother of Jesus. She certainly and unequivocally was the most affirmed woman ever. Look at her unique position among women of all ages: the mother of Jesus the Savior of world. The angel Gabriel, coming from God's presence, greets her: "Rejoice, highly favored one, the Lord is with you; blessed are you among women!" (Lk. 1:28). Let us keep in mind that no matter how much Mary was honored with God's grace, she was not the dispenser   but only the recipient of it. If we go beyond this, we fall into flattery and exaggeration of her proper role. Gabriel's special angelic greeting to her does not stop here, but it extends to the divine affirmation of the Holy Trinity. "The Holy Spirit will come upon you, and the power of the Highest will overshadow you; therefore, also, that Holy One who is to be born will be called the Son of God" (Lk. 1:35).

The pre-incarnate Son of God, in cooperation with His Father and the Holy Spirit, devised a plan to redeem the fallen human race. Jesus offered Himself to be emptied of His divinity, to be born in human form, and to die in our stead. Here Mary receives the affirmation of the three Persons of the Godhead: First, the Holy Spirit would come upon her. Second, the power of the Most High God would overshadow her. Third, the Holy One, the Son of God would be born of her. The fact that Christ wholeheartedly agreed to be conceived in Mary's womb, be nursed, nurtured, and taught by her must have affirmed Mary in the greatest way. He had already agreed to the divine plan, and now the execution of that plan was about to take place.

The Creator Conceived in the Creature!

Let young women imagine the awesomeness of such divine honor bestowed on this young woman. Contemplate the glorious thought that the desire of all the ages, the hope of a doomed world, and the long-awaited Savior was to be formed in the body of a humble young virgin. What a weighty thought that Mary the creature was to carry her Creator in her womb! Let everyone be enthralled with the thought that the living Christ desires to dwell in our hearts today, if we are humble and willing to let Him abide there. This should be a most encouraging blessing to us—to truly believe it and live it.

Another solid affirmation for Mary as a godly mother was that the "Child grew and became strong in spirit, filled with wisdom; and the grace of God was upon Him" (Lk. 2:40). What mother today would not be elated to reap the reward of raising such a quality son? Of course, God was His real teacher working through Mary to implement His will in Jesus' upbringing. What special care must this young mother have taken of her baby boy, knowing that she was raising the Savior of the world! God was His divine instructor, but Mary was His human instructor. "The child Jesus did not receive instruction in the synagogue schools. His mother was His first human teacher. From her lips and from the scrolls of the prophets, He heard of heavenly things" (*The Desire of Ages*, p. 70).

He Honored His Father and Mother

At twelve years of age, Jesus was found in the temple dialoguing with learned teachers of the law. Then after His parents were greatly relieved to find Him, He "went down with them and came to Nazareth, and was subject to them . . .

And Jesus increased in wisdom and stature, and in favor with God and men" (Lk. 2:51, 52). Even after His declaration that He was about His Father's business, He was also about His earthly parents' business of submission to them in respect and loving obedience. And although Jesus realized that He was to love and obey His heavenly Father, yet He did not discharge Himself from loving and obeying His godly human guardians. For about eighteen years after that, He was still respectful and obedient to them.

Many youth of today take their parents for granted, and think that they know much better than them. They think that rendering respect and honor to their parents is old-fashioned and should be taken lightly or discarded altogether. For decades the media had depicted parents in disrespectful caricatures before the young, and now we are reaping the harvest. Consequently relations in the family, society, and with God break down, and many wonder why.

Let the young take a lesson from the perfect Jesus, who knew that He was the divine Son of God, yet considered it a sacred duty and honor to submit to His parents in love and respect, even to the age of thirty and until His death. If Jesus who "increased in wisdom and stature, and in favor with God and men" showed honor to His father and mother, shouldn't we? Not only Jesus showed them honor, but also God showed them great honor in entrusting them with His only Son. This affirmation of the Father and the Son to Mary (and Joseph) played an important role in cooperation with the Spirit in Jesus' mental, physical, social, and spiritual development.

She Shared in His Ministry

After the death of Joseph, Jesus' widowed mother was present at the wedding in Cana. There she witnessed His first miracle as He inaugurated His public ministry. The very fact that she was there to be relied on, as He ministered to others, shows His need and respect for her. There must have been a mutually close and trusting relationship between them. Notice that she ran to Him for help in this sudden crisis when the wedding party had run out of wine. Even when Jesus referred to her as "woman," He showed her honor and respect. In our Western world such reference may seem a bit cold and even discourteous, but in Christ's culture this was indicative of respect and dignity.

The next thing Jesus said to her was that His hour had not yet come to declare Himself as the Messiah. With all due respect to her and her aspirations for Him as His mother, He had to fulfill His Father's divine plan for His mission—in His own way and time. Her immediate response to Him clearly shows that there was no disrespect or conflict between them. Not only had she turned to Him to confide about the crisis, she also trusted in His ability to deal with it. This is evident when she confidently instructed the servants, "Whatever He says to you, do it" (Jn. 2:5).

This needs to serve as a model to be emulated of how godly families should trust and cooperate with each other in their service to God, and in their relationships with others. As we walk and work with Jesus, let us talk to Him about the challenges and crises that confront us. Fully believing that He is able and willing to help; let us, like the servants at the wedding, do whatever He tells us to do. That was the love, respect, and cooperation Jesus and His mother experienced as they served God together. Such mutual experience was by no means limited to one or two occasions but during His entire ministry. "The life of Christ was marked with respect and love for His mother" (*The Desire of Ages*, p. 90). It was a way of life for Him to affirm her in His loving support and also in His respectful exhortation.

She Shared in His Suffering

Such mutual love and support for each other brought to His mother not only joy and fulfillment but also trial and suffering. Her lot in life was linked with His lot, profoundly impacting her entire life. And she had the unique and enduring honor of sharing in her Son's sufferings from beginning to end. "Throughout His life on earth she was a partaker in His sufferings. She witnessed with sorrow the trials brought upon Him in His childhood and youth. By her vindication of what she knew to be right in His conduct, she herself was brought into trying positions" (*The Desire of Ages*, p. 90).

And the greatest trial of her life was when her heart was wounded and her soul pierced at His crucifixion, in fulfillment of Simeon's prophecy spoken directly to Mary in the temple: "Yes, a sword will pierce through your own soul also, that the thoughts of many hearts may be revealed" (Lk. 2:35). The Greek word for "sword" used here refers to the huge, long sword in contrast with the short one. This must have implied that Mary's suffering was going to be particularly severe and enduring, making an indelible impression on her mind. From the very time that Mary's pregnancy was made public, she was shamed for immorality; and later on her Son was shamed for His illegitimacy. This shared shameful treatment plagued them right to the bitter end.

Naturally Mary, as a loving mother, was reluctant to accept the reality of Simeon's prophecy, and the idea of a suffering Messiah. Jesus endeavored to ease her pain by gradually trying to bring her to accept and prepare for this painful reality, in order to make it less traumatic for her at the end. Now she was facing the ultimate test in a most excruciating way for her and her beloved Son. Regardless of the great risk to her own well-being, she closely followed her suffering Messiah Son to the very end, even to the cross. The alleged shame that stigmatized her and her Son throughout their lives, now was to be culminated with the scandalous shame of execution by crucifixion—the death of the worst criminal.

Behold Your Son!

All the disciples fled for their lives except John. The beloved disciple accompanied this grieving mother through her tortuous steps to the cross. Being widowed and now deprived of her condemned Son's protection, John was there for her, acting as the devoted son she desperately needed at this crucial time. "When Jesus therefore saw His mother, and the disciple whom He loved standing by, He said to His mother, 'Woman, behold your son!' Then He said to the disciple, 'Behold your mother!' And from that hour that disciple took her to his own home" (Jn. 19:26, 27). Moments before Jesus bowed His head and gave up the spirit, He thought of His grieving mother and planned for her care. It was excruciatingly painful for Him to breathe and more so to speak, as He was dying, yet He bravely mustered His last breaths and words to show His undying sympathy and support for her.

The fainting and grief-stricken mother could not keep herself away from the horrific scene of her Son's prolonged agony. There is nothing more painful than for a loving mother to helplessly watch her innocent child's protracted anguish. Yet the mutual pain keenly felt by both could not deter Jesus from providing for His mother what she needed most—John, a loving and devoted son like Himself. This was the ultimate affirming support the dying Jesus wanted to bestow upon His mother. "In His dying hour, Christ remembered His mother . . . O pitiful, loving Saviour; amid all His physical pain and mental anguish, He had a thoughtful care for His mother! He had no money for which to provide for her comfort; but He was enshrined in the heart of John, and He gave His mother to him as a precious legacy" (*The Desire of Ages*, p. 752).

Mary Magdalene. Among all the women associated with Jesus and His ministry, this Mary stands out the most in the Gospel narratives. Her experience with Jesus was the fulfillment of His words that to whom much is forgiven, the same loves much. (See Lk. 7:47). Her desperate soul finally found the One whom her heart longed for. The only One who could relieve her of her crushing guilt, forgive her of her many sins, shatter the bondage of demonic power in her life, and by His encouragement and support transformed her to be one of the closest and most devoted of His followers. Let us highlight the occasions when Jesus reached out to her with His enabling affirmation.

Identification and Transformation

Mary is identified as a sinner (Lk. 7:37), with the specific sin of adultery. Her sinful accusers threw her at Jesus' feet ready to stone her to death. Yet they oddly did not think they deserved the same punishment for their own adultery. To this day in some parts of the world, adulterous men cruelly stone women accused of adultery, and they themselves move on without any penalty. How did Jesus deal with this injustice in His day? He leveled the playing field, showing fairness and equality before the law. The just Judge of everyone said: "He who is without sin among you, let him throw a stone at her first" (Jn. 8:7). By this He showed her that she should not be the only one singled out.

When all of her accusers left her alone, Jesus addressed her as a "woman," signifying His respect and validating her dignity as a human being. Then He encouraged her by saying: "Neither do I condemn you; go and sin no more" (Jn. 8:11). He encouraged her because His approach was not to condemn but to save. Jesus came to save people from their sins. "For God did not send His Son into the world to condemn the world, but that the world through Him might be saved" (Jn. 3:17). First, Jesus *validated* her as a woman despite her degraded state. Second, He *identified* with her plight of being condemned. In His loving identification with this condemned woman, soon He Himself was about to be condemned to the cross in her place. Second, by His grace He actually *transformed* her. His precise purpose of validating her and identifying with her was to transform her from a life of sin to a life of righteousness. He believed in her against all odds, that with His help she could be a victor over her besetting sin, and not a victim. That is very uplifting to a crushed spirit!

Jesus wants us to know that affirming others merely for the sake of identification ought not to be an end in itself. Being transformed into His image is the evidence that genuine repentance and forgiveness have taken hold in the life. Many people interpret and apply this text erroneously: in a disorderly, imbalanced, and incomplete way. The proper way to look at this text is to focus on its order, balance, and completeness. *Order* in the sense that the no condemnation part comes before the no sinning part. We cannot tell people to overcome their sins without first telling them about Christ's forgiving and transforming love. It just does not work. *Balance* in the sense that we should not go to the extreme of focusing on one part to the exclusion of the other. *Complete* in the sense that we use the whole text and not just a part of it.

Seven Demons Cast Out

Luke describes Mary Magdalene as one "out of whom had come seven demons" (Lk. 8:2; see also Mk. 16:9). It never ceases to amaze me of how differently Jesus views sinners. Today Mary would be considered a very "high-maintenance" church member, as I unfortunately hear some troubled people being referred to. It is so affirming that Jesus sees the possible in the impossible and the hopeful in the hopeless. She was hopeless to everyone, except for Jesus, that is.

For Jesus, if there is life there is hope. No case is too difficult for Him to deal with as long as we humble ourselves, submit to Him, and walk with in His ways. If the number seven represents perfection, then Mary had a perfect problem with oppressive demons controlling her life. But Jesus had the perfect solution: His love was so powerful that it could shatter the fiendish stranglehold of all the demons combined.

The sort of support Jesus gave Mary did not consist merely of kind and encouraging words, but of the eternal Word that recreated her into His likeness. "Mary had been looked upon as a great sinner, but Christ knew the circumstances that had shaped her life. He might have extinguished every spark of hope in her soul, but He did not. It was He who had lifted her from despair and ruin. Seven times she had heard His rebuke of the demons that controlled her heart and mind. She had heard His strong cries to the Father in her behalf. She knew how offensive is sin to His unsullied purity, and *in His strength she had overcome.* When to human eyes her case appeared hopeless, Christ saw in Mary *capabilities* for good. He saw the *better traits* of her character. The plan of redemption has invested humanity with *great possibilities,* and in Mary these possibilities were to be realized. Through His grace she became a partaker of the divine nature" (*The Desire of Ages,* p. 568, emphasis supplied).

Doing a Beautiful Thing to Jesus

Wouldn't it be greatly encouraging to hear Jesus compliment us with the words that we have done a beautiful thing to Him? Of course it would. But that is exactly what Jesus longs to say in affirming us, if we follow Mary's example of devotion. At Simon's house the disciples severely scolded Mary for her act of devotion. But Jesus stood up for her to defend her with these words: "Let her alone, why do you trouble her? She has done a good work for Me" (Mk. 14:6). I like the way the NIV renders it: "She has done a beautiful thing to Me." How did she do such a beautiful thing to Jesus? And how can we today do likewise? Jesus answers our question: "She has done what she could." Therefore when from the heart we do our part, when we do what we can, and when we do our best, He calls it something good and beautiful. This may not be good enough for some church members, or this may not be even good enough for us, but if it is good enough for Jesus, then it is indeed good enough.

Mary's act of devotion was from a heart overflowing with genuine love for her Master. She offered her noblest service at His feet. In the biblical culture, the noblest part of the body is the head, and the humblest part is the feet. She was not the hostess at Simon's house, yet her great love for Christ helped her succeed where Simon failed. She had no basin, but she had her eyes. She had no water to wash His feet, but she bathed them with her tears. She had no towel to dry His feet, but she dried them with her long hair. She could not stop kissing His feet, yet Simon was not willing to kiss Him on the cheek. Mary ministered to Jesus with her eyes, her tears, her hair, and her lips—all in the head area—at His feet. In a sense she was telling Jesus that she was not worthy to be in His presence, yet she felt honored to serve Him with her best at His feet.

Our Able Advocate

You notice that with all the unjustified and harsh criticism leveled against Mary, she did not become defensive. In fact she remained quiet, because Christ was defending her. I am convinced that the more defensive we become the less we experience Christ's defense in our behalf. If our great Advocate, the Lord of Lords, is defending us, then why do we worry so

much about people's criticism of us? Jesus defended her by
saying: "Leave her alone. Why do you trouble her?" In other
words, how dare you harass her like this especially after she
has done such a beautiful thing to Me? No doubt this was
a most affirming kind of defense Mary was blessed with. As
defendants in the court of the cosmic great controversy, we
will be attacked by the arch-accuser and his cohorts. Let us
resist defending ourselves before them, but appeal to our able
Advocate to answer their attacks. If a defendant can say to his
accusers, "See my lawyer," then we certainly can tell the devil,
"See my Lawyer!" Jesus is more than a match for Satan, and He
can vanquish him speedily.

Anointing Christ's Body

The Holy Spirit prompted Mary to anoint the body
of Jesus for burial. By doing so, she was fulfilling the Old
Testament type of anointing a sacrificial lamb, by anointing the
Lamb of God to be shortly sacrificed on the cross. Paul affirms
this fulfillment in Ephesians 5:2 when He writes: "And walk
in love, as Christ also has loved us and given Himself for us,
an offering and a sacrifice to God for a sweet smelling aroma."
What great honor and high compliment Christ conferred on
Mary by sanctioning her ministry to Him in this sacred fashion!
"She has come beforehand," Jesus affirmed, "to anoint My
body for burial" (Mk. 14:8). "Christ delighted in the earnest
desire of Mary to do the will of her Lord. He accepted the
wealth of pure affection which His disciples did not, would not,
understand . . . It was the love of Christ that constrained her . . .
The ointment was a symbol of the heart of the giver. It was the
outward demonstration of a love fed by heavenly streams until
it overflowed" (*The Desire of Ages*, p. 564).

The Fragrance of the Gospel

As the alabaster box was broken, and the precious fragrance

of the nard pervaded the house, soon the body of Jesus was to be broken on the cross and saturate the world with the sweet aroma of the Gospel. No power could keep Mary's spilled nard from inundating the house, and no power was going to stop the fragrance of the Gospel from permeating the entire world. Jesus greatly affirmed Mary by perpetually linking her devoted act with the spreading of the Gospel. "Assuredly, I say to you, when this gospel is preached throughout the whole world," Jesus declared, "what this woman did will also be spoken of as a memorial to her" (Mk. 14:9). What a tremendous honor from Christ bestowed upon a forgiven sinner, whose act of devotion was to be a constant memorial for the diffusion of the message of salvation! "Kingdoms would rise and fall; the names of monarchs and conquerors would be forgotten; but this woman's deed would be immortalized upon the pages of sacred history" (*The Desire of Ages*, p. 563).

One Thing Needed

In the Luke 10:38-42 narrative we learn about two godly sisters with two different temperaments. Jesus lovingly addressed both sisters in love when He said: "Martha, Martha, you are worried and troubled about many things. But one thing is needed, and Mary has chosen that good part, which will not be taken away from her." There we have the dutiful Martha who was eager to provide the best hospitality for Jesus. She showed her love for Him by preparing the tasty food. On the other hand we have the affectionate Mary who showed her love to Jesus by providing the needed fellowship.

Food and fellowship are both important for us, but which must take the priority? Sharing in fellowship with Jesus should come before partaking food with Him. That does not mean a meal should not be prepared; it needs to be, but it should not be too elaborate ant time-consuming. Food is eaten a few times every day, but how often does Jesus come to visit? Wouldn't it be tragic to expend most of the time in food preparation and little time in fellowship with Him!

Mary learned the valuable lesson of making sure that first things came first, the other things would work out accordingly. Let us say that food represented what was of temporary value, and fellowship with Jesus signified what was of eternal worth. Mary had learned the valuable lesson her Master taught in Matthew 6:33. "But seek first the kingdom of God and His righteousness, and all these things shall be added to you." God wants to give us His kingdom and also all the other important things in life. We would be big losers if we focus only on His wonderful gifts, but not on the wonderful Giver. But when we focus on His kingdom and righteousness we are winners; for in making sure of the first priority, the rest follows suit. It is like a life-giving breath we take, which is vitally important for all our good accomplishments.

Marthas are certainly needed today, but they need to first make sure of their saving relationship with Jesus, and then let all their service flow out of such a relationship. Jesus drew a clear contrast between the "many things" with the "one thing." There are altogether too many good distractions, but there is only the one true attraction, Jesus. As the old chorus goes, "Turn your eyes upon Jesus, look full in His wonderful face, and the things of earth will grow strangely dim in the light of His glory and grace." The subtle deceiver loves to sidetrack us with good and even spiritual activities in order to distract us from Jesus. It is incredible, isn't it, that we can be distracted from the Master Teacher in our good teaching, sidetracked from the Wonderful Counselor in our helpful counsel, diverted from the Great Physician in restoring the sick, and be deflected from the Faithful Witness in our successful witnessing. This all depends on our focus and priority. Don't we want our first and foremost priority to fellowship with Jesus, to receive His righteousness, and to inherit His kingdom?

Maybe it is not readily apparent that Jesus not only affirmed Mary, but that He also affirmed Martha. In His encouragement, He reached out to both of them on their own level. Martha loved Jesus also in her own way, and was the one who invited Him to the house to spend time with her sister Mary and her brother Lazarus. Jesus was endeavoring to lead her closer in her walk with Him. He was glad that Mary was at His feet, but encouraged Martha to look beyond her gracious hospitality to her gracious Lord. Notice that He gently called her name twice, "Martha, Martha," implying His affection, caring, and concern for her. Thus He validated her in order to bring her up higher in her ongoing spiritual walk with Him. You can imagine Jesus opening His heart to her and helping her focus on lasting priorities. And as far as He was concerned, fellowshipping with her was more important than the tastiest of foods.

It should be very heartening to know that Jesus loves and values us for our sake. He relishes being in the company of those who love Him and delight to obey Him. Contemplate these moving words about how greatly Jesus values genuine human relationships. Notice that He desires with all His heart to relate to you as He related to Mary, Martha, and Lazarus, if we simply open our hearts to Him. "He loves all the human family, and to some He is bound by peculiarly tender associations. His heart was knit by a strong bond of affection to the family at Bethany. . . Here He found a sincere welcome, and pure, holy friendship. Here He could speak with simplicity and perfect freedom, knowing that His words would be understood and treasured. Our Saviour appreciated a quiet home and interested listeners. He longed for human tenderness, courtesy, and affection" (*The Desire of Ages*, p. 254).

Eyewitness to the Resurrection

In connection with the resurrection, Mary had the sacred honor and unique privilege, more than any of Christ's disciples, of being the first, the last, and the one who lingered around Christ the most. She seems to have been present at any event associated with His death and resurrection from the dead. Mary was present when He was crucified and buried. She was the last one to leave the tomb where He was buried, and the first person the resurrected Christ greeted that glorious morning. She was so wrapped up in her Lord that she simply could not leave Him, no matter what the circumstances were. She must have come very early in the morning to the tomb, for she witnessed the great earthquake caused by the angel who descended from heaven. She witnessed him rolling the stone and sitting on it, and then she saw the fearful guards who became like dead men. She entered and saw the empty tomb, and was told by the angel that Christ was raised from the dead. The angel told her to break the good news of the resurrection to the disciples. While on her way to break the news to them, she met the resurrected Christ and worshipped Him as He personally told her to tell the disciples the good news. Earlier she had encountered the resurrected Christ as she lingered the longest around the tomb. This is the time when she thought He was the gardener, and when He told her not to cling to Him before His ascension to His Father. What great affirmation! More than anyone else, the Lord let her be in the know about the sacred events associated with His glorious resurrection. (See Matt. 28; Mk. 16; Lk. 24; Jn. 20).

The Widow's Two Mites. As Jesus was watching the rich put their money in the treasury, he noticed a very poor widow giving her last two mites—all she had. He called His disciples and said: "Assuredly, I say to you that this poor widow has put in more than all those who have given to the treasury;

for they all put in out of their abundance, but she out of her poverty put in all that she had, her whole livelihood" (Mk. 12:43, 44). She must have lived in abject poverty as a widow, living a hand-to-mouth existence. The rich "put in" much in the temple treasury, but she "threw in" her two mites. She seemed to hesitate in her self-consciousness to be seen with such a tiny gift, that at an opportune moment she simply threw it in and quickly parted.

In His commendation of this humble widow, Jesus draws a sharp contrast between her minute gift and the huge gifts of the rich. First, the mite was the smallest of the Jewish coins at that time, worth a portion of a penny today. Second, it is the motive for giving the mite that counts the most for Christ. A miniscule gift with a pure motive is worth much more than gigantic gifts with selfish motives. Third, Jesus commended her on her spirit of giving all that she had—her entire livelihood. The rich people gave from their surplus, and it cost them nothing—they did not feel it or miss it. In the eyes of the world she gave the least and the rich gave the most, but in Christ's eyes she gave the most and they gave the least.

The Mighty Mites

In practical terms, how then was her tiny gift much more than all the other huge gifts? It is true that one penny with God's blessing is exceedingly more than millions of dollars without His blessing. Not only did Christ commend her motives but also the potential results of her gift. "The influence of that little gift has been like a stream, small in its beginning, but widening and deepening as it flowed down through the ages. In a thousand ways it has contributed to the relief and the spread of the gospel. Her example of self-sacrifice has acted and reacted upon thousands of hearts in every land and in every age" (*The Desire of Ages*, p. 616).

We are also told about Jesus' affirming commendation of her. To teach His disciples a memorable lesson in unselfish giving, He made sure that His encouraging words were heard by her. She was moved to tears of gratitude to hear Jesus' validation and great appreciation of the superb quality and quantity of her sacrificial gift. "The Saviour called His disciples to Him, and made them mark the widow's poverty. Then *His words of commendation* fell upon her ear . . . *Tears of joy* filled her eyes as she felt that her act was *understood and appreciated*" (*ibid.*, p. 615, emphasis supplied). Her act of unselfishness was in a sense similar to Mary's act of devotion—both commended by Christ, and immortalized. "She did *what she could*, and her act was to be a *monument to her memory through all time, and her joy in eternity*. Her heart went with her gift" (*ibid.*, emphasis supplied).

The Woman's Touch of Faith. This miracle of healing the woman long-plagued (twelve years) with the issue of blood clearly shows the sensitive and encouraging heart of Jesus. This is evident in the fact that He was intent on knowing who had touched Him. Also the uplifting words to this suffering woman: "Daughter, your faith has made you well. Go in peace, and be healed of your affliction." (Mk. 5:34).

Again Jesus emphasizes the striking contrast between what a touch of genuine faith can do with what human expertise cannot do. Also, the contrast is drawn between this woman's impossible circumstances and her tenacious doggedness to reach Jesus. A seemingly impossible state of affairs engulfed this poor woman. First, Christ was heavily pressed on all sides by the masses following Him, pushing and shoving. Second, with her weakened condition resulting from bleeding, and her utter emotional despair in being pronounced incurable by many physicians, it is incredible that she kept on trying. Third, she was bankrupt of all her resources, seeking an illusive cure. Fourth, with all her tireless efforts, her condition only worsened. Fifth, she was embarrassed to speak to Christ publicly because of the private nature of her malady. Plus she feared the ritual uncleanness and avoidance associated with her condition.

Audacious Faith

With the high heap of formidable obstacles in her way, it is incredible that she stubbornly kept on trying. But she was so determined in her desperation to reach Jesus that no power on earth was going to hold her back. What forces propelled this woman to go on? She had heard of the Great Physician, and in her distress she wanted to get near Him. Many physicians pocketed all the money she had, only for her condition to worsen. But now her crushed hope was revived by faith in the Great Physician who would heal her completely without any financial cost. That was her one chance as she caught a glimpse of Jesus, and she was determined not to lose it. Her kind of audacious faith was simply unstoppable: "If only I can touch His clothing," she said, "I shall be made well" (Mk. 5:28). And as she reached out in faith to touch Jesus, power flowed out of Him and instantly healed her.

"Daughter"

Besides the great affirmation of her miracle of healing, let us look at the other affirming words of Jesus to her. First, He suddenly stopped in the midst of the choking throng, to the puzzlement of His disciples, to inquire about the touch of someone. Many people were shoving, pushing, and touching Him, but now He unexpectedly stopped to inquire about this one special touch of faith that instantly released His healing power. Second, Christ referred to this fearful and trembling woman as "daughter" (v. 34). He used this endearing and reassuring reference to her to assuage her fear—exactly what she needed at the time. In His sensitivity and compassion, He intended to make her feel accepted as a close family member— even as His own daughter.

Third, Jesus preceded His reference to "daughter" in Matthew's narrative by the heartening words: "Be of good cheer" (Matt. 9:22). She had endured twelve years of misery, and now Jesus wanted to cheer her up as a caring father desires to cheer up his hurting daughter. Fourth, He complimented her genuine and abiding faith in His healing power: "Your faith has made you whole," He gently assured her. No matter how insignificant and weak she may have felt at the time, yet she played a very crucial part in her healing in total trust and cooperation in divine power. Finally, Jesus bid her peace as He moved on, the peace that restored her body and spirit. Shortly before she had nothing but apprehension and anxiety about this dreadful condition, but now the Prince of Peace was there to replace all of that with His peace that passes understanding.

What an amazing and awesome Great Physician and Prince of Peace! Let us confidently trust Him with all our hearts to receive His healing and peace. The disciples, who were puzzled and impatient with their Master for inquiring as to who had touched Him, would learn later on how much they would need this miracle to bolster their courage. "The Saviour could distinguish the touch of faith from the casual contact of the careless throng. Such trust should not be passed without comment. He would speak to the humble woman words of comfort that would be to her a wellspring of joy,—words that would be a blessing to His followers to the close of time" (*The Desire of Ages*, p. 344).

The Widow of Nain. Imagine with me for a moment witnessing that sad funeral procession. The scene was especially sad because of the grieving mother who was left alone to languish in her loneliness and lack of family support. After all, she was already widowed, and soon she was to bury her only son, her only source of sustenance in her old age. It is recorded that "When the Lord saw her, He had compassion on her and said to her, 'Do not weep'" (Lk. 7:13). Jesus' heart was moved to the core for this destitute widow as He saw her blinded with tears and tragedy. When He saw her, He saw her with His heart, and this kind of seeing moved Him to show compassion for her.

To Suffer With

The word "compassion" literally means to suffer with. This clearly implies that Jesus was not at all a passive spectator, but an engaged participant in this widow's tragic loss. He was vicariously suffering her loss as if her deceased son were His own. This affirming compassion stirred Him to do two things that totally transformed the whole tragic scene into a joyous celebration. One, He uttered these sympathetic words, "Do not weep" (v. 13). Two, He acted by raising him from the dead (v. 14). As we say today, "Actions speak louder than words." It is easy for people to say encouraging words, but they often cannot do a thing to ameliorate the situation.

We frequently hear the words: "Keep your courage up," and "Don't worry, everything will be alright." But not so with Jesus, for He not only speaks but implements what He says. His words are living and creative. He was about to change the widow's sorrow into joy. He not only cares but He also can. He is able to do all that He desires. Imagine that scene of hopelessness when Jesus drew near to the open casket, touched it, and commanded the dead son, "Young man, I say to you, arise" (Lk. 7:14). Then the dead son was made alive through Christ's resurrection power as he sat and began to speak. That was the most precious and desperately needed gift Christ could ever give to this grieving mother. He transformed her tears of sadness to tears of joy.

That is the kind of wonderful Savior we have in Jesus! His big heart is full of compassion, encouragement, and support.

DISCUSSION QUESTIONS

1. How do you view John 8:11 in a balanced and complete way? What difference does this make in how you understand and apply it? How can Christ's approach of identification for the sake of transformation be useful to you in affirming others?

2. Reflect on this statement: The more we feel the need to defend ourselves the less we experience Christ's defense in our behalf. How is this so?

3. How do you explain the fact that the widow's gift of a mere mite was of a better quality and quantity than all the others? How does this affirm you when you give from your heart in the best way you can?

4. In what ways did Christ affirm the audacious faith of the woman who touched the hem of His garment? Jesus called her "daughter." What does this imply? How would you feel if Christ referred to you as daughter or son?

5. What does it mean that Jesus not only feels with you but He also shares in your suffering? Jesus is not only available but also able and willing to do something about your predicament. In what way does this bolster your courage?

CHAPTER SIX

Affirming Foreigners

"So Jesus answered and said, 'Were there not ten cleansed? But where are the nine? Were there not any found who returned to give glory to God except this foreigner?' And He said to him, 'Arise, go your way. Your faith has made you well'" (Luke 17:17-19).

The sight of a young missionary's hands tending the decaying flesh and binding the oozing wounds of a leper in Africa etched an indelible memory in my mind. She said that her calling in life was to extend Christ's touch of compassion to the "least of these." Believing that she was doing this for the love of her Lord, she lovingly and patiently tended the men at the leprosarium. Now and then she would venture out with fellow workers to salvage abandoned lepers, dumped by the side of the road, left to suffer and die. After a brief visit to that leprosarium and seeing those horrible sights, I felt faint and sick to my stomach, feeling the need to take a break from it all.

But the missionary nurse was touching these lepers with her own hands, day in and day out, and with a smile, too. They were not her countrymen, not from her race, her religion or culture. They were not only total foreigners to her, but also rejected outcasts in their own country. The lepers felt that the loving care of this dedicated missionary was almost too good to be true, and the only thing they could do was to say thank you very much over and over again. This was a living demonstration of what Christ is like. When He met the leper, as recorded in Mark

1:40, 41, He was "moved with compassion, put out His hand and touched him, and said to him, 'I am willing; be cleansed.'"

One Grateful Foreigner. The above mission experience reminded me of Jesus healing the ten lepers, and deliberately pointing out that one of them was a foreigner. Luke's narrative specifically indicates that he was a Samaritan. Jesus cleansed all of the ten lepers, but "one of them, when he saw that he was healed, returned, and with a loud voice glorified God, and fell on his face at His feet, giving Him thanks. And he was a Samaritan" (Lk. 17:15, 16). The Samaritans then were definitely despised even more than foreigners. They were considered a half-breed racially and religiously. They were the descendants of a mixture of Babylonian and Jewish ancestry of the exilic years. They were loathed as traitors, detested as collaborators with their enemies, and shunned as heretics. The Jews always regarded them with suspicion and distrust, and had no dealings with them whatsoever.

These ten lepers—nine Jews and one Samaritan—found themselves pulled together by their mutual misery and their common need for healing. They all must have had faith when Jesus told them to go and show themselves to the priests; for on their way there they were all cleansed. The faith that was exercised by the nine healed lepers did not express itself in gratitude, however. Maybe as Jews they felt some entitlement to the miracle as children of Abraham. It was quite apparent that they were so fixated on their cleansing that they forgot about their Cleanser. God's blessings can draw us closer to or further away from Christ, depending on what we choose to focus on. Happily the one foreign leper chose to focus on the Blesser and not solely on the blessing. That is why he was not carried away with the miracle, but was drawn toward the Miracle Worker. For it is obvious that there would be no miracle without the

One to make it happen. In his humility he felt undeserving of the healing; therefore he did not take it for granted, but received it with great gratitude.

Gratitude and Ingratitude

When we are in a crisis we plead with God to answer our prayer requests. We fervently and frequently pray, and even fast as we implore Him to meet our needs. But when God answers our prayers, do we remember to thank Him? Do we thank Him right away, or do we remember by chance to thank Him later on, if at all? The one leper was so full of gratitude that he immediately went back to praise the Benefactor. Let us in summary contrast the reaction of the one compared with the nine. First, realizing that they were healed, the nine went on their merry way; but the one leper, in his exhilaration, overlooked going to the priests first, as he was told; instead He went straight away to Jesus. Second, in his exuberance he glorified God with a loud voice. He was so excited that he could not contain his intense feelings of thankfulness. Third, he praised God not only with his voice but also with his actions. He fell down on his face at Jesus' feet—the ultimate expression of humility and gratitude in the biblical culture. Fourth, he expressed his heart-felt thanks to Jesus.

Christ, in His regard for and affirmation of this Samaritan man, makes him stand out in contrast with the other nine, as an excellent example of expressing gratitude. Also, Jesus clearly indicates that it does matter to Him if we express gratitude where it is justly due. Obviously Jesus was not insecure and needing some compliment from others, but because He well knew that the expression of thanks would have a positive impact on the unthankful recipients. Ingratitude can do detrimental things to us, affecting our lives for the worse. It helps us to take God's blessings for granted. It promotes the attitude of entitlement toward such assumed blessings. Ingratitude reinforces the Santa Claus mentality about God. We push certain buttons, and there come the goodies. It stifles our spiritual growth by drawing us away from Christ, and by making us more self-centered. It holds God back from pouring out His special blessings upon us, not because He does not love us but because He is careful not to see His generosity towards us become counterproductive.

Expression and Suppression of Gratitude

The suppression of gratitude is not conducive to our total well-being, physically, mentally, and spiritually. In the book, *The Ministry of Healing*, pages 251-253, we find several benefits for expressing gratitude and praise to God. One, there is "nothing that tends more to promote health of body and of soul than does a spirit of gratitude and praise." Two, words of gratitude can impact our thoughts and character; for our positive expression can create a new reality on the ground of affirmative thought patterns that enhance our character development. Three, it is a "law of nature that our thoughts and feelings are encouraged and strengthened as we give them utterance. While words express thoughts, it is also true that thoughts follow words." Four, regardless of our carelessness in expressing gratitude, let us "educate our hearts and lips to speak the praise of God for His matchless love."

It is never too late to retrain our minds to establish fresh patterns of thought. And we can be assured that Christ, who delights in giving us encouragement and in receiving our gratitude, is always there to help us. His greatest miracle of cleansing is the cleansing from the deadly leprosy of sin. May He when He comes around to ask, "But where are the nine," find you and me giving glory and gratitude to Him, just like the one grateful leper.

The Syro-Phoenician Woman. "O Woman, great is your faith!" These are Christ's encouraging words to the Canaanite woman, spoken from a heart deeply stirred and pleased by her unwavering faith. She comes across as a fitting fulfillment of Hebrews 11:6, which says: "But without faith it is impossible to please Him, for He who comes to God must believe that He is, and that He is a rewarder of those who diligently seek Him." In fact, her great faith did please Jesus and propelled Him to give her such a great commendation. Her faith was unflinching in Jesus' love and in His ability to reward her heart-felt earnestness.

This woman was a Gentile born in Syro-Phoenicia which is in present-day Lebanon, bordering the region of Galilee. She must have heard of the great compassion Jesus showed in healing the many sick and suffering ones who came to Him. Mark's narrative says that "she heard about Him" (7:25). She was also keenly aware that she and her people were hated by the Jews who thought of them as less than despicable dogs. A current saying among the Jews at the time was that God created the Gentiles to fuel the fires of hell. This foreign woman must have had a lot of unusual spunk to brave such formidable obstacles to seek help from Jesus. In her motherly love for her demon-possessed daughter, and finding no relief anywhere, she was desperate to go to any length to seek help.

But behind all this background, the most powerful impetus for her was the wonderful things that she heard and believed about Jesus; and now it was her golden opportunity to find out for herself. Moreover, "Christ knew this woman's situation. He knew that she was longing to see Him, and He placed Himself in her path" (*The Desire of Ages*, p. 400). In essence, she wanted to see Him and He wanted to see her—an unbeatable combination! This was her one and only chance, and she was not by any means going to squander it. If she did not receive help from Jesus, she was not going to receive it from anyone else, for sure. That is why she was doggedly determined not to leave, under any circumstances, until her desperate need was met. She was indeed seeking Jesus with all her heart.

Her determination was evident as she approached Jesus, because she cried out to Him and repeatedly begged Him to deliver her daughter from her tormenting demon. Risking the annoyance and disgust of the disciples, she had the nerve to persevere and go nowhere else until she received the help she was desperately seeking. Jesus saw the prejudicial hearts of His disciples, and He wanted to teach them an indispensable lesson of viewing such Gentiles as precious human beings created in God's image, and not as despicable dogs. And it was not too early to learn this needed and valuable lesson if they were going to reach the Gentiles with salvation. Also, Jesus wanted to plainly reveal to all around this stranger's humility, trust, and appreciation of what she believed Christ was going to do for her. He wanted them to clearly see how her tenacious faith was to be severely tested; and how she was going to pass that test with flying colors, putting to shame many of the unbelieving children of Israel.

Of Crumbs and Dogs

In His wise approach, Jesus seemed to go along with the prevailing prejudice of the disciples in order to contrast His loving approach with their cold manner, and her humble character with their pride and prejudice. And this Syro-Phoenician woman proved to be an excellent instrument in Jesus' hands, not only to bless her but to bless so many others with the good news of salvation. Let's look at her responses to the challenges put before her, and the reasons why Jesus gave her such a hearty commendation:

First, "He answered her not a word." Simulating how the

Jews would have treated this foreign woman, Jesus seemed to ignore her fervent plea even though she called Him Lord and Son of David. Giving her the silent treatment, He moved on as if she had said nothing to Him. But she apparently believed that what Christ had in His heart for her was more than He seemed to outwardly convey. It seemed as if she were giving Him the full benefit of the doubt, so to speak. She kept on pursuing Him and crying out for help.

Second, the disciples mistakenly thought that Jesus approved of the accepted way of dealing with her lot. So they urged Him to "Send her away, for she cries out after us." Jesus did not send her away, and she stubbornly stayed on.

Third, Jesus said to her and to the disciples: "I was not sent except to the lost sheep of the house of Israel" (Matt. 15:24). In deftly feigning the heartless exclusivity of the Jews, He sounded as if the Gentiles were excluded from the blessings reserved only for the children of Israel. This served only to make her entreaties more earnest. Considering Him Lord, she bowed and worshiped Him with the simple and straightforward supplication: "Lord, help me!" (v. 25). She definitely did not take no for an answer.

Fourth, Jesus still pressing the way the Jews would have treated her said something that could have defensibly discouraged a Gentile with a weaker faith, but not her. "It is not good to take the children's bread and throw it to the little dogs" (v. 26). The Jews who despised this woman as a despicable dog, not deserving of any blessing, were themselves conspiring to kill Him. The so-called children, who shamefully viewed this woman as a dog, were treating Jesus the opposite way than she herself was. She believed in Him, they disbelieved in Him. She acknowledged Him as Lord and the promised Son of David, they disavowed Him as such. She worshiped Him as her Lord; they accused Him of blasphemy for accepting worship. His love drew her ever closer toward Him, but they pulled themselves further away from Him.

Fifth, the stark differences between what was considered a despised Gentile dog and a cherished child from the house of Israel were quite revealing. Not intending to disappoint dog lovers in the Western culture, dogs were considered (and still are) in that part of the world to be half-wild, filthy, vicious scavengers. They were never treated as pampered indoor pets like they are today. To level an insult of calling someone a dog was most demeaning. Dogs were considered unclean and nearly on the same low level as swine. Both were grouped in the same category and were parallel to each other, as seen in Matthew 7:6. "Do not give what is holy to the dogs; nor cast your pearls before swine." This point was clarified to show how much Jesus was impressed with the woman's unrelenting faith. He tightened the screws around her faith even more, only to rebound stronger than ever.

"Great Is Your Faith!"

Sixth, she did not even mind being viewed as a dog if that was going to help her hopeless daughter. "True, Lord, yet even the little dogs eat the crumbs which fall from their master's table" (Matt. 15:27). She was not reluctant to go along agreeing that she was as a dog, as long as she was granted the chance of a little dog to eat the little crumbs that fell to the floor. Pride and prejudice played no part in her pleas because of her implicit faith in Christ, and her desperate need which she believed He would surely fulfill. "Let the children of the house of Israel have the most bountiful and sumptuous feast, if they so wish," she may have thought. "But I have no problem with what they feel they are entitled to, as long as you let me have the crumbs."

Seventh, the climax of all of this was the exuberant commendation of Jesus: "O woman, great is your faith! Let it be to you as you desire" (v. 28). Jesus was so impressed with her indomitable faith that He seemed unable to restrain Himself from exclaiming in affirming love and sympathy in our jargon: "Right on, woman! Your faith is awesome!" He was hard pressed to even find such faith among His own disciples, not to mention the Scribes and Pharisees. Many barriers and obstacles were placed in the way of this heathen woman, but "there are no barriers which man or Satan can erect but that faith can penetrate. In faith the woman of Phoenicia flung herself against the barriers that had been piled up between Jew and Gentile. Against discouragement, regardless of appearances that might have led her to doubt, she trusted the Saviour's love" (*The Desire of Ages*, p. 403).

The Great Faith of the Centurion. This heathen Roman officer serves as a powerful demonstration of God's grace to change lives. In spite of all the prejudices surrounding him on all sides, he was able somehow to see a genuine picture of what Christ was like and the truth He taught about God. We have already discussed the other two foreigners whom Christ affirmed: the leper from Samaria, and the woman from Syro-Phoenicia. Now we will consider what led Christ to give this heathen Roman centurion such commendation for his great faith. Notice that the three persons in the order already mentioned get further away from the Jewish people religiously, racially, and geographically: Samaria, Syro-Phoenicia, and now Rome. This Roman centurion was not only considered a total Gentile who was steeped in heathenism, but a visible representative of the oppressive Roman power—a heathen conqueror living in the midst of conquered Jews.

A Righteous Roman

Before Jesus commended him for his great faith, surprisingly the Jews actually liked him and commended him for his many good qualities. As intermediaries (as the custom was and still is), they recommended him to Jesus as worthy for his dying servant to be healed. After all, he had done a lot of good things for them: "And when they [Jewish elders] came to Jesus, they begged Him earnestly, saying that the one for whom He should do this was worthy [of healing his servant], for he loves our nation, and has built us a synagogue" (Lk. 7:4, 5).

Politically and religiously he was quite favorable to the Jews: politically, he loved their nation; and religiously, he had built them a synagogue. Probably this man was acknowledged as a "proselyte of the gate," meaning that he believed in God and the teachings of His people, but he did not fully convert to Judaism. Here we have a hint of Jewish legalism. They focused only on his good works for worthiness before God, but Jesus focused on His living faith that led to good works.

Notice that this centurion, who could have been cruel, haughty, abusive, and oppressive, was just the opposite: charitable, humble, and feeling unworthy. All his earnest pleas and the pleas of others were focused on one thing: getting his servant healed. This is also quite unusual to have such a quality relationship between a master and a servant, considering how servants or slaves were treated at the time. This is another clear indication that the transforming grace of the God of Israel in Whom he believed had been effectual in his life. Moreover, in his feeling of unworthiness, he sent one after the other, to recommend him to Jesus: the Jewish elders and his friends. The elders commended him, and his friends conveyed his feeling of unworthiness. Feeling unworthy that Christ would come under his roof, or for himself to go to Christ.

It is interesting to note that the Jews themselves felt worthy, and they tried to make him worthy like themselves (for favors rendered). But he and his own friends emphasized his unworthiness. When we have a genuine relationship with

God, we are humbled and feel undeserving of His goodness. Our focus is not on self and our worthiness, but on Him and His worthiness. We feel our desperate need for God, and thus experience His transforming power in our daily lives.

The genuine humility of the centurion and his feeling of total lack of entitlement were combined with his implicit faith in Christ's ability to do the impossible. He clearly did not need any further proof or persuasion; neither did he need any lingering doubt to be dissipated. He simply believed in the infinite power of God's word that commands the world into existence, and still sustains it. Such potent word could certainly heal his wonderful servant. And to make sure that his utter and unqualified faith was precisely known, he said that Jesus did not have to bother coming or going, "but say the word, and my servant will be healed" (Lk. 7:7).

A Marvelous Faith

Then the centurion used his own experience as a commander of soldiers to clinch his case. What he was in essence saying was: if he as a centurion—a mere human being—could expect total obedience to his word from his soldiers, how exceedingly more was the supreme Commander of the universe able to execute His sovereign will. We can imagine how pleased Jesus would have been if He had witnessed such expression of genuine faith among His people.

But alas such faith was not to be found, and that is why when "Jesus heard these things, He marveled at him, and turned around and said to the crowd that followed Him, 'I say to you, I have not found such faith, not even in Israel!'" (Lk. 7:9). Imagine this: Jesus commended the faith of this heathen centurion above all the faith He could find among the chosen people of Israel. No wonder Jesus intended His commendation to the centurion to be a public one, to serve as a living example of extraordinary faith for others to emulate. That is why He turned around, as He marveled at him, to commend him before the crowd that was following Him.

It is not often recorded that Jesus "marveled" at something or somebody, but in this case He did. Wouldn't it be so affirming to have Jesus marvel at our strong faith in Him? To "marvel" means to experience serendipitous amazement and admiration at something. Jesus greatly desires to marvel at our faith; and this can become a reality as we humbly submit to Him, linking whatever measure of faith we have with His omnipotent faith.

This narrative is concluded in Matthew 8:11, 12 with an additional detail not found in Luke. Jesus here connects the marvelous faith of this foreign centurion with the faith of the many that "will come from east and west, and sit down with Abraham, Isaac, and Jacob in the kingdom of heaven" (v. 11). The commendation of the centurion is prophetically linked to the commendation of the countless others from heathen lands that will have the faith to follow Him. Such divine commendation does not result from our race, nationality, or status, but is the result of implicit faith and trust in our Savior, and the Savior of the entire world.

The Samaritan Woman.

In the Middle Eastern culture of today, as it was at the time of Jesus, to give a drink of water to the thirsty is a must out of a sense of sacred duty. You even extend this favor to an enemy, for water is considered life and a hallowed gift from God. Therefore, to ask for a cold drink of water to quench one's thirst is to build a good rapport with the giver. Before any sort of salutation was extended to the Samaritan woman who came to draw water, Jesus immediately asked her for a drink of water. In this significant encounter at Jacob's well, Jesus used a most bold and radical approach to affirm her as a foreigner, and to draw her to the well of salvation.

The Hated Samaritans

We need to understand the background of this encounter to appreciate even more what Jesus was trying to accomplish. In their pride and exclusiveness, the Jews looked down at any one who was not a child of Abraham, yet in their estimation the Samaritans were considered the worst of all. It was a long-running family feud that was so deeply entrenched that seemed impossible to resolve. In John 8:48 we clearly see how loathsome the Samaritans were to them. In their vindictive hatred, the Jews lumped Him together with the Samaritans as they were conspiring to murder Him. They said to Him: "Do we not say rightly that You are a Samaritan and have a demon." They hurled at Jesus the most hurtful and hateful thing imaginable to them. They associated being a Samaritan with being demon-possessed. Thus they considered them as the worst specimen of humanity (Samaritan), and the worst specimen before God (demon).

Earlier, it was mentioned that in the biblical culture then and today, a cold drink of water was normally given even to an enemy. But a drink of water was not to be given to a Samaritan according to Jewish tradition. The only thing allowed was trade, but only when it was expedient or essential. Here are some informative comments from *The Desire of Ages,* page 183. "The Jews and the Samaritans were bitter enemies, and as far as possible avoided all dealing with each other." Personal and social contact of any kind was "condemned." As far as receiving or giving any help or favor, a "Jew would not borrow from a Samaritan, nor receive a kindness, not even a morsel of bread or a cup of water." Even Christ's disciples were swept away by this antagonistic culture that they were brought up in. For them to "ask for a favor from the Samaritans, or in any way seek to benefit them, did not enter into the thought of even Christ's disciples."

Christ's Affirmation of the Samaritans

Jesus charted a brand new and bold course in reaching out to the despised Samaritans. In doing so, He was demonstrating before His disciples how to break loose from this prejudicial bondage that they were so accustomed to. Soon He was going to need them to help Him seek and save those who were despised and lost. It is a fact that prejudice produces prejudice, and distrust disseminates distrust. Consequently, the implacable state of prejudice and distrust among both groups was mutually experienced, and it was getting worse and worse. "Though He was a Jew, He mingled freely with the Samaritans, setting at naught the Pharisaic customs of His nation. In face of their prejudices He accepted the hospitality of this despised people. He slept under their roofs, ate with them at their tables,— partaking of the food prepared and served by their hands,— taught in their streets, and treated them with the utmost kindness and courtesy" (*ibid.*, p. 193).

There is nothing more affirming or complimentary, nothing more engendering of trust, than the way Jesus related to the Samaritans. He accepted their hospitality in several effective ways. First, He slept in their houses—a very trusting gesture which says He felt safe and secure with them. Second, He ate their food prepared with their own hands. Eating at their table implied social closeness and spiritual bonding with them, particularly when the meal was prepared with their hands— it was like a gift of themselves that Jesus gratefully accepted. Although eating out with friends at a local restaurant today is easy and convenient, yet it would not be the same as eating a meal at their home, prepared and served with their own hands.

Third, He treated them with the utmost sensitivity, politeness, and respect as He associated with them.

"Give Me a Drink"

"A woman of Samaria came to draw water. Jesus said to her, 'Give Me a drink'" (Jn. 4:7). What a personal and direct request made of even a Samaritan woman! He asked for a favor, not offered one. When we carefully reflect on Jesus' affirmation of this woman, we notice that He did so not only in word but also in deed. First, in His verbal affirmation He talked to her as a friend, for He plainly confided in her that He was the awaited Messiah, and that His salvation was for her and her people. He was often reticent to tell anyone, especially the Jewish leaders, about Him being the awaited Messiah for fear of their misconception, rejection, and opposition.

Second, He won her trust as He spoke the truth in love about her situation and the way of salvation. Third, even though He could have said a few things about her sinful life, He focused on what could be construed as truth in her response about having no husband. "You have well said," Jesus said to her, 'I have no husband,'" (Jn. 4:17). Fourth, in His genuine love Jesus maintained a balance of striving to save her soul and yet not glossing over her struggle with sin. Fifth, He was reciprocal in His approach to her: He needed her to satisfy His physical thirst, and she needed Him to quench her spiritual thirst.

Christ's affirmation indeed started firstly by asking her for a favor, not offering her one. "The King of heaven came to this outcast soul, *asking a service at her hands. . . .* He was *dependent* upon a stranger's kindness for even the gift of a drink of water" (*The Desire of Ages*, p. 184, emphasis supplied). In that culture, asking for and receiving a favor makes the receivers vulnerable to the givers. It opens them up to expectations, reciprocation of the favor, and even indebtedness. There was not supposed to be even a casual contact between the Jews and Samaritans, and here Jesus went so far as to ask for a favor that one would ask of a friend.

Secondly, He showed in action that He was bold enough to defy the established traditions of a Jewish *man* talking publicly to a Samaritan *woman*. It was bad enough to have man-to-man contact, but Jesus went way beyond that to speak to a Samaritan woman. That is why in her shock she pointedly asked: "How is it that You being a Jew [Jewish man], ask a drink from me, a Samaritan woman?" (Jn. 4:9). The disciples revealed their Jewish traditions, for upon their return they were astonished too that He was talking to her (Jn. 4:27).

Thirdly, Jesus who attracted multitudes of people vying for His attention and clamoring for His help, reserved special time for this one woman, a special one-on-one audience with her. He made her feel special and validated by having a heart-to-heart conversation with her.

Spiritual Food and Drink

Another surprise for the disciples: their Master's hunger was for some reason satisfied. They went to town to get their hungry Master some food, but instead of finding Him famished, they found Him satiated. The reason for Him not being hungry was because He had partaken of a superior food: "My food is to do the will of Him who sent Me, and to finish His work" (Jn. 4:34). It is interesting to take note of the two surprising things that occurred. The woman, in her excitement, did not do what she had come to do. She forgot to draw water, she forgot to take her water pot with her, and consequently she forgot to give Jesus the drink of water He had asked for.

The other surprising thing was that the thirsty and hungry Jesus was neither thirsty nor hungry anymore. For the joy of quenching her thirst with the water of life was indeed His food and drink. Thus in affirming her He received affirmation from her: she received Him as her Savior. "As His words to the woman had aroused her conscience, Jesus rejoiced. He saw her drinking of the water of life, and His own hunger and thirst were satisfied" (*The Desire of Ages*, p. 191). We all experienced at some point losing our hunger when engrossed in a task we are passionate about. This Samaritan woman would have felt quite commended to know that Jesus was so thrilled and gratified by her response that He felt no need for the meal brought to Him by His disciples.

DISCUSSION QUESTIONS

1. Jesus recognized the gratitude of the one leper and the ingratitude of the other nine. What does this tell you about Jesus? What does it tell you about the one and the nine healed lepers?

2. Why did Jesus use the Jewish approach of associating the Syro-Phoenician woman with dogs? What does her unusual response tell you about the kind of faith she possessed?

3. Why were the Jews so impressed with the Roman centurion? What role did their high recommendation play in the healing of his servant, if any? Would Christ have healed the servant anyway? Why, or why not?

4. How would you utilize Christ's approach in asking for a favor from the Samaritan woman in your witness to ostracized people?

5. The Samaritan woman left without water, and did not offer Jesus the drink He asked for. And although Jesus was hungry, He did not eat the food His disciples brought Him. Explain all of these surprising outcomes. How would you apply this to yourself and your affirming witness?

CHAPTER SEVEN

Affirming the Erring

"I say to you that likewise there will be more joy in heaven over one sinner who repents than over ninety-nine just persons who need no repentance" (Luke 15:7).

As members of the human race we all err at one time or another, for to err is human. This is an incontrovertible fact of existence that we all have in common. The crucial issue here is not whether we err, but rather how we relate to the erring, be it us or others. There is no greater example than that of Jesus who knew exactly how to affirm, exhort, and encourage the wayward ones. He treated such with genuine kindness, not mistaken kindness; and with genuine love, not misguided love. Yes, Jesus was truly kind and loving to the erring, but He also encouraged them to rise above their circumstances, and held them accountable to fulfill His expectation of trusting and obeying Him. His responsible dealing with the erring was a far cry from the permissive ways of our post-modern age.

The word *balance* comes to mind when we reflect on Christ's approach to this sensitive issue of dealing with the erring. There is often a tendency to go to extremes: either harsh condemnation or irresponsible commendation. But Jesus loved sinners in order to transform them; and He was gracious to them so that they might be empowered to become overcomers. The sinners whom Christ tried to help may be divided into two groups. One is humble and responsive; the other is haughty and resistant. You see, our human reaction to Christ's initiative is critical here. Do we respond to Him positively, or do we resist Him persistently? That is indeed the determinative question.

Peter's Setbacks and Comebacks. Peter serves as an encouraging and prime example of the humble and responsive group. No matter how many times he stumbled in His spiritual walk, He nevertheless stuck it out with Jesus, and was made an overcomer. Let us trace some of Peter's setbacks and see how Jesus turned them into comebacks.

Discouraged by the malice and opposition of the Jewish leaders during Christ's difficult mission in Judea and Nazareth, Peter left Jesus to go fishing with a few of his fellow disciples. In addition to this, the continued imprisonment of John the Baptist haunted him as the possible prospect of casting His lot with Jesus. So he went back to his old reliable standby, what he was good at: making a living at fishing. But Peter failed miserably in his fishing expertise, trying all night but catching nothing. At the moment of extreme failure and discouragement, Jesus showed up and told him to go out and try again. No word of reprimand or recrimination from Christ's lips, but words of confidence that success was at hand.

"At Your Word"

And true to form, Peter questioned Christ's command but then trustingly agreed to obey it. "Master, we have toiled all night and caught nothing; nevertheless at Your word I will let down the net" (Lk. 5:5). Often Christ can reach us best when we are at our worst. We become humble and dependent on Him when we fail at the only thing we are good at. Therefore, in trusting Jesus, sure success emerges out of dismal failure; for we are left with nowhere to turn except to Him. At the sight of this amazing miracle of the big catch, Peter felt his unworthiness to be in the presence of his pure and powerful Master Fisherman. Love for his Lord sprang up afresh in his heart as he realized his waywardness in leaving Jesus' side in fishing together for souls. He left Jesus but Jesus never left him. The Lord came pursuing him with care and hope for greater things.

Totally overwhelmed by this marvelous miracle, Peter in his feelings of humility and unworthiness threw himself at Jesus' knees saying: "Depart from me, for I am a sinful man, O Lord!" (Lk. 5:8). Christ's affirming love and care stirred Peter's heart to leave all things behind, and run to Jesus, not wanting to part with Him. "Do not be afraid," Jesus encouraged him. "From now on you will catch men" (v. 10). As if Jesus was reassuring His disciple: "If you rely on Me, I not only can give you success in catching fish, but much more importantly success in catching people for the kingdom." He raised his vision ever higher— from total failure in catching fish to success in saving souls. "It is Satan's work to discourage the soul; it is Christ's work to inspire with faith and hope" (*The Desire of Ages*, p. 249).

In throwing himself at Jesus' knees, Peter in essence was saying to Him, how can You tolerate being around a sinner like me, but I am so glad You are still here with me. Notice this holy tension in Peter's heart, telling Jesus to leave him yet to remain with him. Leave him, because he felt so undeserving; not leave him, because he desperately needed His Master. This moment of truth, this point of holy tension is a commendable position to be in. Even though he asked Jesus to leave him, "yet he clung to the feet of Jesus, feeling that he could not be parted from Him . . . Peter had been led to self-renunciation and dependence upon divine power that he received the call to his work for Christ" (*ibid.*, p. 246). Before Peter saw a true picture of self and service, He was struck by a vision of His merciful Savior. Only as we see what Jesus is really like can we truly see what we are like. From this essential and holy tension springs forth the vision of service.

Sinking and Saving

Also there was the unforgettable experience of Peter walking on water, as described in Matthew 14:25-31. He was afraid of Jesus, thinking He was a ghost; then he walked on the waves with Him; then he was afraid again and started sinking; and finally he was rescued when he cried out for Jesus to save him. How was Jesus affirming to Peter and his fellow disciples, as their boat was being tossed by contrary winds? He did not abandon them to their own fate, but were always on His mind and in His heart. "Not for a moment did He lose sight of His disciples. With deepest solitude His eyes followed the storm-tossed boat with its precious burden; for these men were to be the light of the world. As a mother in tender love watches her child, so the compassionate Master watched His disciples" (*ibid*., p. 381).

Jesus boosted their courage and dispelled their fear with His uplifting words: "Be of good cheer! It is I; do not be afraid" (Matt. 14:27). Then the impulsive, risk-taking Peter challenged His Master saying that if it was really Him, to let him walk on the water. Jesus gave him a simple command to come, and Peter walked on the water all the way to where He was standing. He could have scolded him for needing confirmation that He was indeed Jesus. He simply placed His faith in Peter to walk to Him, as long as he kept his eyes focused on Him. He was not to focus on the waves or look back at the other disciples. Nevertheless he was distracted from Christ and began to sink; and immediately he cried out for Jesus to save him.

Again Jesus did not scold him, but stretched forth His hand and lifted him to safety next to Him. Caringly Jesus exhorted Peter to have more faith by saying: "O you of little faith, why did you doubt?" (Matt. 14:31). Peter's confidence in self could have been ruinous without learning the essential lesson of self-distrust and Christ-trust. Patiently and gradually Jesus helped him learn the crucial lesson that at the point when he thought himself strong, he was weak. He knew that Peter's faith was sometimes unstable, leading him to doubt; but He had high hopes for him to grow in his faith as He learned to increasingly focus on Him. He desired that Peter would anchor his weak faith in His mighty faith, and that He would let such faith dispel any doubt and darkness.

Likewise, Jesus has high hopes for each one of us regardless of our struggles. Although He knows our weaknesses, yet He believes in us against all odds; that in depending on Him we can become overcomers. He affirms us by cheering us on life's journey, speaking hope and courage. He reminds us again to look unto Him and be saved from discouragement and despair. Imagine Him saying to us: "Look up unto Me and live; look down and away from Me and fail." Therefore, let us look up and live! Peter could have given up by giving way to his doubt, but instead he looked up unto Jesus to save him. He bids us, His modern-day disciples, not to give up but to look up.

"I Have Prayed for You"

There was the occasion when Jesus affirmed Peter in praying for him as recorded in Luke 22:31, 32. Jesus well knew that His erring disciple seemed contradictory and extreme in his character. Yet He was totally devoted to fashion his character in His likeness. He was, what we might call, a difficult student but a willing and teachable one. On occasions he could be courageous and cowardly, bold and vacillating, humble and boastful, generous and selfish. If Jesus was so willing to see his potential, and was so committed to build up his character, no doubt He would be eager to work on us, if like Peter we would be humble and willing. When He prayed specifically for him He had his character defects in mind. He knew that the terrible trials that would test His disciple to the core were just on the verge of his Master's trial and crucifixion.

Christ's Way of Affirmation

As Jesus told Peter that Satan was after him to sift him like wheat, He also assured him that He was supporting him with His prayers, which were designed to defeat all of Satan's attacks. "But I have prayed for you, that your faith should not fail; and when you have returned to Me, strengthen your brethren" (Lk. 22:32). Affirmation is seen in Christ through His care and commitment to fervently pray for Peter. He also had a yearning hope and optimism that Peter's faith would not fail if he kept his eyes on Him. Unfortunately Peter was not that receptive to Christ's prayers in his behalf. And even though Jesus knew that in his weakened spiritual state he would deny Him, yet He held out hope for him not only to repent but to also encourage others.

Remember that right after this, as recorded in Luke 22:33, Peter pledged himself to suffer and even die for the Master he sincerely loved. By His encouraging approach, Christ was intentional in not letting His erring disciple wallow in regret and despair for his cowardice and broken promises. In his earnestness he declared: "Lord, I am ready to go with You, both to prison and to death." But just before thrice denying His Lord, Peter was the one who encouraged his fellow disciples to flee for their lives. He was so grieved that the cause was lost, seeing that Christ decided to undergo suffering and death. "In their indignation and fear, Peter proposed that they save themselves" by scurrying for safety (*The Desire of Ages*, p. 697). He ominously helped fulfill the prophecy in that "they all forsook Him and fled" (Mk. 14:50).

Christ desired to lift Peter's narrow sight beyond his cowardice, denials, and ensuing discouragement to genuine repentance and restoration. He also wanted him to know that *in spite of everything* He still needed Him to minister to those in need of His salvation. Imagine for a moment Christ's unwavering faith in and hope for His beleaguered Peter. This is in spite of the fact that in quick succession he violated his repeated pledges, he encouraged all to take flight to save their necks, and he vehemently denied his Lord three times with swearing and cursing. In Christ's mind the now weak Peter was going to be strong in Christ soon after, to even strengthen the weak ones to be strong in Christ as well.

One Glance

In this sorry state of disloyalty and degradation, a condemning glance from Jesus could have easily crushed Peter with despondency. But to the contrary, Jesus' look was a look of compassion and acceptance, not a look of anger and condemnation. In the midst of His own suffering when He could not speak words of encouragement, He still turned and looked at him with pity and sympathy. That glance, full of grace, embarked Peter on his journey of recovery and restoration.

There was so much packed in that one glance. That loving look quickly awakened many memories of how Jesus related to him and his fellow disciples when they had erred. "A tide of memories rushed over him. The Saviour's tender mercy, His kindness and long-suffering, His gentleness and patience toward His erring disciples,—all was remembered" (*ibid.*, p. 713). His remorse was so profound and his tears so bitter that in a daze he found himself in Gethsemane. There he fell upon his face and wept bitterly, wishing he could just die. In a sense he was reliving His Master's agony when He took him along with James and John to share in the sorrow of His soul. There in the same place Jesus "began to be troubled and deeply distressed." Then He confided in them that His soul was "exceedingly sorrowful, even to death," and exhorting them to "Stay here and watch" (Mk. 14:33, 34).

What an interesting turn of events! The very thing that Jesus urged him to do, but which he was unprepared to do, he was now ready to retrace his halting steps back to the same hallowed ground to stay, watch, and pray. As Jesus was praying and agonizing alone now Peter was doing the same, wishing he could have been close to Jesus then and there. "It was torture to his bleeding heart to know that he had added the heaviest burden to the Saviour's humiliation and grief. On the very spot where Jesus had poured out His soul in agony to His Father, Peter fell upon his face, and wished that he might die" (*The Desire of Ages.*, p. 713).

There was Jesus' compassionate glance on Friday morning. This was the last time Peter saw Jesus and the last thing he remembered. Then that glance toward Peter was affirmed by a word about Peter early Sunday morning. The resurrected Lord desired that Mary and the other women "go and tell His disciples—and Peter—that He is going before you into Galilee" (Mk. 16:7). Peter was most likely the disciple who suffered the most that weekend. Full of regret and remorse, he spent long hours brooding over what he considered a despicable denial of His loving Lord.

Although he remembered Christ's compassionate and forgiving look, in his feeling of unworthiness he needed the encouraging reassurance that indeed he was forgiven. And now the resurrected Lord had him specifically on His mind by singling him out by name to hear the good news of the resurrection. This was the desperately needed assurance that Jesus still loved Peter dearly, and that He had graciously accepted his true repentance, and had magnanimously forgiven him.

"Do You Love Me More than These?"

Now we come to the third time when Jesus met with His disciples (seven of them) before His ascension to heaven. (See John 21:1-22). Christ had already appeared to them on two other occasions, and by now it dawned on them that Christ was soon to ascend to heaven. So again they followed Peter's proposal to go fishing with him. Going fishing this time was not because of discouragement, but because they wanted to put food on the table and replenish their dwindling resources. They usefully occupied themselves while waiting to receive their mandate to preach the gospel under the Pentecostal anointing of the Holy Spirit.

Yet it seems evident that Christ had a special concern for Peter this time. In the Bible lands then, and even now, there was this tradition of shame and honor. Dishonor and grievances had to be dealt with properly, and could not be shoved under the rug, so to speak. Unfortunately, there isn't much of this mindset in our Western culture today, where Christians who dishonor God and others are less likely to feel remorse about wrong acts committed. Peter still felt deeply the dishonor he brought upon Jesus, the shame he brought upon himself, and the distrust he incurred on his fellow disciples. And even though he knew that Jesus had forgiven him, yet there were consequences to his actions: wounds to be healed, damage to be repaired, and trust to be restored. Christ wanted to help him restore his trust among the disciples so that they would have confidence in his leadership; thus his ministry would be successful for the cause of Christ.

It is encouraging that Christ was so committed to this restoration process that He was quite devoted in actualizing it before He ascended to heaven. He loved Peter, believed in his potential, and needed him to be a mighty apostle for Him. Peter needed to know that Jesus still loved him, that he was still cherished in His heart regardless of what had transpired. So Jesus directly asked him three times, corresponding with his three denials, if he loved Him. In His first two questions Jesus used the Greek verb *agapao*, which refers to the highest type of love, the love that is unconditional and is controlled by durable principle not wavering emotion. In His last question to Peter, He used the Greek verb *phileo*, which refers to the spontaneous brotherly love among friends.

Jesus' questions reflected the priorities that He had for His disciple: the mutual love for each other. The divine love and brotherly love that He wanted to assure Peter of. It must have been quite validating for him to realize that his Master desired to love him as His God and as His Friend and Brother. In the first question asked: "Simon, son of Jonah, do you love Me more than these?" (Jn. 21:15) Jesus included the phrase "more than these." Here Jesus affirmed Peter by wanting him to love Him more than anyone else or anything else. If he drew genuine love from Him the Source of love, it would flow out of him to others in abundance. In this way he would be more able to love and feed Christ's sheep and His lambs. Jesus entrusted him with His precious flock of new believers as well as the more mature ones. That was exactly what Peter was hoping to hear that despite his shameful acts, Christ was eager to commission His disciple to carry on His sacred work of ministry.

The whole emphasis in this encounter is on love as the first and foremost criteria for service. Our service to Christ must always issue forth from our love to Him, not the other way around. For what is the significance of any kind of Christian endeavor unless it is conceived and nurtured in love? In the personal and final encounter with Peter, Jesus repeated the question about loving Him three times for emphasis. This question must apparently be of most crucial significance to Christ and to us. It is the "only condition of discipleship and service. . . . This is the essential qualification. Though Peter might possess every other, yet without the love of Christ he could not be a faithful shepherd over the Lord's flock. Knowledge, benevolence, eloquence, gratitude, and zeal are all aids in the good work; but without the love of Jesus in the

the heart, the work of the Christian minister is a failure" (*The Desire of Ages*, p. 815).

Love unto Death

Apparently Jesus took Peter aside for a One-on-one conversation. He really wanted to convey to him, not only before the disciples, but to him personally how willing He was to trust Peter—even to die for Him the death of crucifixion. Like He trusted John the Baptist to die the death of a martyr, He also had confidence in Peter to be martyred on a cross for His sake. It is revealing that what Peter pledged but failed to do for Jesus' pre-resurrection, he succeeded in doing post-resurrection. He pledged to suffer, go to prison, and even die for his Master, but he did not. But Christ gave him another opportunity to prove himself and to fulfill this pledge, and he did just that with flying colors. He suffered for Christ, went to prison for His sake, and died for Him even on a cross.

"Most assuredly, I say to you, when you were younger, you girded yourself and walked where you wished; but when you are old, you will stretch out your hands, and another will gird you and carry you where you do not wish. This Jesus spoke, signifying by what death he would glorify God" (Jn. 21:18, 19). What a great honor to commend Peter in such a way, that He would know that this staunchly loyal apostle would love Him to the extreme extent of paying the ultimate sacrifice in heroically glorifying Him. Thus faithful Peter would not only "strengthen" his brethren in life but also in death. Many future martyrs would be bolstered with courage looking back at the faithful example of Peter.

Love: Does It Help or Hinder?

Satan, the great deceiver, is always thrilled to talk about love as long as he talks about it in the wrong way. He is quite skilled at taking the most wonderful and godly virtues and twisting them to his liking. Thus many are deceived without even knowing it. The virtue of love is one of the most misunderstood virtues in our times. Particularly when it comes to loving the erring, many Christians want to shower their love carelessly without any expectation, accountability, or exhortation. They heave such so-called love on them, so irresponsibly, that their spiritual growth is actually hindered and not helped.

This love is misguided, and emboldens in wrong doing; it may be sincere, but sincerely wrong. Notice the difference between Christ's responsible love and our misguided love. He lovingly corrected Peter and held him accountable, but never left him to wallow in his own fate. Also Peter, although struggling and reproved, stuck it out with Jesus; and neither one abandoned the other regardless of difficult circumstances.

Christ's exhortations are designed to show His caring and love, His wounds are intended to heal and restore, and His warnings are meant to give encouragement and hope—all such is the stuff of which genuine love is made of. Those who practice superficial and misguided love do not possess the courage to speak the truth in love, for fear of being criticized or rejected. Whatever compromise or appeasement it takes to maintain a relationship with others, they stubbornly latch on to for dear life. "Jesus reproved His disciples, He warned and cautioned them; but John and Peter and their brethren did not leave Him. Notwithstanding the reproofs, they chose to be with Jesus. And the Saviour did not, because of their errors, withdraw from them. He takes men as they are, with all their faults and weaknesses, and trains them for His service, if they will be disciplined and taught by Him" (*Education*, p. 91).

The following example associates the relationship of our children to us as parents, and our relationship to our heavenly Father. Take careful note of what constitutes genuine love and misguided love. "The child who loves his parents will show that love by willing obedience; but the selfish, ungrateful child seeks to do as little as possible for his parents, while at the same time desires to enjoy all the privileges granted to the obedient and faithful. The same difference is seen among those who profess to be children of God. Many who know that they are the objects of His love and care, and who desire to receive His blessings, take no delight in doing His will. They regard God's claims upon them as an unpleasant restraint, His commandments as a grievous yoke. But he who is truly seeking for holiness of heart and life delights in the law of God, and mourns only that he falls so far short of meeting its requirements" (*The Sanctified Life*, p. 81).

The Chief Tax Collector. Another notable example of Jesus correctly affirming the erring is shown in how He dealt with Zacchaeus. This rich tax collector was what we would call today a tax commissioner, having other tax collectors working under him. The Roman tax collection system encouraged greed and extortion, and Zacchaeus took full advantage of this to amass ill-earned riches. With the backing of the power of Rome, he extorted more money than the law would allow in order to keep it for himself. Consequently, he was hated for being a traitor to his nation for selling out to the oppressive Romans, and was also despised for being an extortionist of his own people. After all, tax collectors are not usually the most liked or popular people anyway. Add to that the shameful stigma of treason and extortion—a combination for a very unsavory character, to say the least.

Could Jesus help and restore such a hated person? Even if he genuinely moved towards repentance, others stereotyping him would make it extremely difficult for him to walk the path to recovery. Yet when Jesus passed by his hometown of Jericho, a glimmer of hope began to shed light on his path as he rushed to see a glimpse of the Redeemer; so much so that he did not mind the indignity of climbing up a sycamore tree. Nothing was going to impede his desire to see the loving face of his only Hope. Many among the pressing throng would not even mention his name on their lips, not wanting in anyway to be associated with him. But by publicly calling this man, short in stature, by name, Jesus launched a series of steps in finally bringing him and his household to salvation.

Affirming Steps in Restoration

"And when Jesus came to the place, He looked up and saw him, and said to him, 'Zacchaeus, make haste and come down, for today I must stay at your house'" (Lk. 19:5). Here we see that even before calling him Jesus saw him. So we can say that Jesus' **first** winning step in restoring this fraudulent tax agent was to look up and see him. Many of his countrymen looked passed him or away from him, and did not want to recognize his presence by making eye contact with him. But on the contrary, Jesus loved him enough to intentionally look up and see him face to face. The **second** winning step was Jesus calling him by name in order to personally validate him and make him feel special.

The **third** step the Lord used was to urge Zacchaeus to quickly come down and stand by Him. By this generous act He was showing that He was not embarrassed to be seen with him, and wanted the whole onlooking crowd to see that He was squarely on the side of this erring man. Jesus clearly indicated that this redemptive relationship was so crucial to Him that He wanted it to happen immediately. There is absolutely no need for any delay on the part of Jesus when a humble sinner desires to connect with Jesus. For indeed "the Son of Man has come to seek and to save that which was lost" (Lk. 19:10).

Jesus' **fourth** step in reaching out to this erring soul was that of taking the unusual liberty of inviting Himself to this tax collector's house. This is the only narrative in the Gospels that records such an initiative. In that part of the world, even till this day, if one is invited for a meal at someone's house, he is to be invited with insistent prodding. It would not be proper for the invitee to readily accept such an invitation, for such quick response would show him to be quite gullible and ill-mannered. Only close family members can initiate inviting themselves. Therefore by inviting Himself to Zacchaeus' house Jesus was clearly showing that He considered him a close family member. And by so doing He was deliberately going out of His way to reveal how much He cared to save this sinful publican.

What prompted Zacchaeus to look for Jesus and to respond to Him so willingly? Earlier he had heard about John the Baptist and his call to repentance. He had also heard of Jesus' kindness and love for despised people like himself. Gradually his heart became receptive to the promptings of the Spirit to change his wayward ways. "He knew the Scriptures, and was convinced that his practice was wrong. . . . Yet what he had heard of Jesus kindled hope in his heart. Repentance, reformation of life, was possible, even to him" (*The Desire of Ages*, p. 553). His mindset corresponded exactly to his eager response to Jesus' initiative. It is recorded that he "made haste and came down, and received Him joyfully" (Lk. 19:6), precisely as Jesus had instructed him, and he did it with a receptive heart full of joy.

His repentance was the genuine type that the Baptist had preached about, because it wrought true reformation. In the presence of the Lord this tight-fisted and greedy sinner became open-handed and generous. The treasure of having Christ as his newly-found Friend outweighed all his other treasures. He willingly offered to give half of his possessions to the poor, and to those whom he might have defrauded to restore fourfold. Like the apostle Paul, he counted "all things loss for the excellence of knowing Christ Jesus" (Phil. 2:8).

Fifth, Jesus finally pronounced the good news to this forgiven tax collector and his house: Jesus said to him: "Today salvation has come to this house, because he also is a son of Abraham" (Lk. 19:9). Presumptuous and dangerous notions abound which lead people to surmise that God's love is so great that He forgives unconditionally without confession of sin and desire to abandon it. Following Jesus from the heart always brings about reformation of character and transformation of life. "No repentance is genuine that does not work reformation. The righteousness of Christ is not a cloak to cover unconfessed and unforsaken sin" (*The Desire of Ages*, pp. 555, 556).

Holding on to unconfessed and unforsaken sin clearly implies that such a darling sin is more valuable to us than holding on to Jesus. But what partnership does Jesus have with sin? Of course, He generously forgives sin that is confessed and forsaken, but He cannot and will not tolerate it in our lives. "Satan deceives many with the plausible theory that God's love for His people is so great that He will excuse sin in them. . . . The unconditional pardon of sin never has been, and never will be" (*Patriarchs and Prophets*, p. 522). The extreme of dwelling only on God's love to the exclusion of the essential human response to His appeals is misleading and perilous. "The religion which makes of sin a light matter, dwelling upon the love of God to the sinner regardless of his actions, only encourages the sinner to believe that God will receive him while he continues in that which he knows to be sin" (*Testimonies,* vol. 5, p. 540).

From Socialization to Salvation

We may summarize the above process that Jesus followed in saving Zacchaeus in these four winning ways (the four S's): One, He *Socialized* with him. This was his immediate felt need for social acceptability. He was greatly affirmed that Jesus Himself possessing the most pristine reputation and impeccable character wanted to be his friend and family. Two, He *Sympathized* with him. As Jesus socialized with him in his home He became more acquainted with him as a person with a heart trying to be liberated from the bondage of degradation and sin. Sympathy filled His heart for this struggling son of Abraham, and He longed to redeem him for His kingdom. Three, He *Served* him in meeting his needs, especially the deeper ones. He caringly ministered to him in validating his heart-felt testimony and determination to set things straight. Four, Jesus *Saved* him and his household. Here we see a vivid demonstration of how Jesus restored this erring one by first being people-oriented, then task-oriented.

"Am I My Brother's Keeper?"

Especially in our post-modern culture, people are inclined to resist any helpful counsel even if it is spoken in love. Many seem to exhibit extreme individualism and self-centeredness. Narcissism is fast becoming a national epidemic. Everything rotates around one's self, and self becomes the demigod to be worshipped. This manifests itself in deciding what you want to do in life without regard to anyone or to any norm. There is the bewitching compulsion to craft your own preferred personhood without any conformity to any examples, even good ones.

Consequently, you do not. want anyone to have any expectation of you, thus allowing you to do what you like to do without any accountability. And even though such self-centered behavior offends or hurts others, it does not matter, for one has to be himself not being concerned about what others think or expect. This detached and callous approach hearkens back to Cain, who wanted to do his own thing regardless of its offence to God, disappointment and hurt to his godly parents. All of this ended in the tragic murder of his innocent brother Abel. After all the damage his selfish attitude caused, he coldly told God, "Am I my brother's keeper?"

The Cains of today place themselves in such situations that it becomes extremely difficult for them to be humble and repentant. There is no question that God loves all rebels with longsuffering and compassion, but the time comes when by deliberate and consistent defiance they close their hearts to His love. There are examples of such erring persons in the Scriptures who willfully disregarded God's loving appeals over and over again. Lucifer was the first example of this. Judas was another, as well as Saul. In the lukewarm church of Laodicea, if this intolerable condition persisted, Christ would spew (vomit) them out of His mouth (Rev. 3:16). Ephraim in the book of Hosea is another example. The more God reached out to him in love the more he pulled away from Him, until finally God said, "Ephraim is joined to idols, let him alone" (Hos. 4:17).

Christ stands at the door of every heart knocking and pleading for us to open to Him, but He will stay outside unless He is invited in. "Christ sees that which man does not see. He sees the sins which, if not repented of, will exhaust the patience of a long suffering God. Christ cannot take up the names of those who are satisfied in their own self-sufficiency. He cannot importune in behalf of a people who feel no need of His help, who claim to know and possess everything" (*Review and Herald*, July 23, 1889).

Eventual Capitulation

In our age this arrogant defiance against godly authority and counsel is reinforced when the erring insist on their wrong course, assuring themselves that their opponents will eventually come to sympathize with them and support them. And this is precisely what happens all too often, thus enabling the erring and emboldening them to persist in their ways in anticipation of eventual support. Thus we indulge them and ourselves in this hazardous, misguided love, and in this pretentious, mistaken kindness. We may imagine we are helping such for the moment but in reality we are hurting them instead. This is because they are not held to any standard or accountability, and there is no fear of any consequence to their willful actions. Such promotes irresponsibility and boldness in pursuing a wrong course of action regardless of its outcome. In this totally self-centered way, they come to expect that the world will come their way if they simply persist.

These days it is fashionable, yet tragic, that our self-centered culture leads people to believe that they can do anything they desire without regard to anyone or anything. It is popular to go against authority, even that which is ordained by God. If youth are not taught by precept and example to honor father and mother, then they are less likely to show respect to their teachers, pastors, significant others, and consequently not even to God Himself. It is acceptable today to go against parental counsel, to shun godly advice, and to disregard divine principles. Yet such erring ones are quite attentive to those companions who agree with them and enable them in their waywardness.

Itching Ears

We can see clearly such phenomenon in Paul's counsel to Timothy regarding those who have haughty hearts and itching ears. Paul's prediction in 2 Timothy 4:3, 4 is certainly being fulfilled today. "For the time will come when they will not endure sound doctrines, but according to their own desires, because they have itching ears, they will heap up for themselves teachers; and they will turn their ears away from the truth, and be turned aside to fables." The erring ones described here are not those whose hearts are open to godly counsel or exhortation to change their ways. On the contrary they are determined to persist in their ways no matter what.

That is why they cannot stand hearing God's counsel for it contradicts their willfulness.

They may even pretend to be godly by twisting God's counsel to fit their own selfish desires. And to solidify their sinful ways they gather around them as many as possible, and only those who would sympathize and enable them in their independent ways. They are so entrenched in what they want that they usually prove to be extremely difficult to be humble and teachable before God. The most loving and affirming counsel of Christ or His servants goes unheeded, and it takes a big upheaval or a major crisis in their lives to possibly turn them around.

In his epistle to Timothy, Paul talks about "perilous times" that would come upon humanity before Christ's coming. He recounts all the rebellious characteristics of the last generation. (See 2 Tim. 3:1-5), then he concludes in verse five with the sad admonition: "And from such people turn away!" To turn away from such persons seems hard and unloving, but they gradually become so hardened that only God can deal with them. The most loving and helpful thing to do under the circumstances is to turn away from them, but not before turning them over to God—this is a divine burden that belongs to Him. Also, we must continue to pray for them in the hope that they may truly repent and turn to God.

Following Christ's Counsel of Matthew 18. Jesus tells us clearly in Matthew 18:15-17 how to relate to a fellow church member who injures us or sins against us in some way. There are four consequential steps in Christ's wise counsel; and if such an approach is faithfully followed, everyone would be spared a lot of trouble. Such a balanced approach minimizes misunderstanding and keeps us from the extremes of pampering the offender or being harsh and arbitrary. It is wise that such a delicate balance be always kept in mind.

Affirming the Erring

The First Step of Restoration

The first step is to go to the offending brother *alone*, one-on-one, and tell him about the problem. "Moreover, if your brother sins against you," Jesus counsels, "go and tell him his fault between you and him alone. If he hears you, you have gained your brother" (v. 15). The first thing we must do in applying this wise approach is to show love and respect towards the offender as an individual in order to avoid any misunderstanding and gossip, and protect his privacy. To hear first hand and directly from us about our genuine concern for our erring brothers or sisters can be affirming. It shows consideration, respect, and thoughtfulness, and thus can starve a fire from its oxygen.

This private conversation must be kept strictly confidential while our best efforts are put forth to lovingly resolve the issue at hand. The good news is if he heeds your counsel "you have gained your brother," and have saved him and the church from a likely embarrassment and possible escalation of the problem. When this step is not thus followed, tragic consequences can occur. I am sure many of us are familiar with church members and even spiritual leaders, who talk about a troubled brother or a sister among groups of friends, without first reaching out privately to that brother or sister. This is in direct opposition to Christ's clear counsel, and should be stopped.

The Second Step of Restoration

The second step to follow is if he does not cooperate with you, then take with you one or two more persons to help reason with him, and to serve as witnesses. "But if he will not hear you, take with you one or two more, that by the mouth of two or three witnesses every word may be established" (v. 16). Again the emphasis is not on broadcasting the problem to the whole church, but in limiting it to a very small group of two or three persons. Hopefully he would cooperate with them and thus the problem would be amicably resolved. It is also prudent to have such persons accompanying you be witnesses to help keep everyone involved in this delicate process honest, unbiased, and accountable as to what transpires.

Moreover, the one or two persons, not involved in the case, can be objective and effective in counseling the wrongdoer, thus increasing the chance of helping the injured party. It is also wise to remember that in these sensitive circumstances there are always two sides to a conflict. Here both sides can be heard, giving them the opportunity to be dealt with fairly in a give-and-take interaction. Again what is discussed should be kept strictly confidential among those few trusted members, while doing everything possible to remedy the situation before it is appealed to a higher level, taking on a wider scope.

The Third Step of Restoration

The third step, if your fellow church member refuses to cooperate with the small group, then take the matter up with the church in a board meeting or later in a business session, if needed. The church must exercise its capacity and authority as the body of Christ to reason lovingly and responsibly with such a member. This now represents a much larger group of fellow believers giving him counsel. Hopefully the large number of church members agreeing together and voicing their counsel would stir up his heart to reconsider his entrenched position. But if he is so self-absorbed that he disregards not merely a few but the many, then this must move the church to administer further redemptive discipline.

The whole church and its mission is undermined when a member's independent and stubborn misbehavior is treated lightly or overlooked. When such a member resists the counsel of the church, he then resists all the members of the body of Christ. This now involves the whole church, and its God-sanctioned responsibility should be seriously exercised. This is done for the purpose of not only redeeming the erring brother, but also of protecting the purity and reputation of the church.

The Fourth Step: Redemptive Discipline

Finally in the fourth step, the Lord continues with His counsel: "And if he [your offending brother] refuses to hear them, tell it to the church. But if he refuses even to hear the church, let him be to you like a heathen and a tax collector" (v. 17). Now the situation takes on more ominous consequences because this erring brother refuses all personal and corporate counsel. It is clear that by his resistant attitude he has separated himself from Christ and His body of believers. This question now begs to be answered is: What does Jesus mean in saying to treat such a one as a "heathen or tax collector"? We know how Jesus treated them when they were receptive to His entreaties of love, repentance, and restoration. But even for the publicans, Pharisees, and heathens who deliberately rejected His entreaties, separating themselves from Him, He still prayed and hoped that their hardened hearts would be softened in repentance.

Like a Heathen and Tax Collector

The heathens and tax collectors were avoided in every way, and no attempt was made to have any interaction with them. But the separation of brothers and sisters from the church, after all efforts are deliberately and consistently resisted, does not mean that we should cease from loving them, praying for them, and keeping all avenues open for their repentance and restoration. The brother in Matthew chapter 18 was not at all remorseful or repentant; but hope must be kept alive for a genuine comeback.

However, we should resist the extremes of hating him on one hand, or coddling him as if nothing had happened, on the other hand. To treat him as a severed member as any outsider, is to show concern for him over his deliberate sinful behavior, in the hope that he will miss his former fellowship with the church. If we indulgently dote on him we are in danger of seeming to treat sin as of no consequence, and appearing to share his errant views and practices. A deliberate and persistent sinful behavior should never be rewarded under the guise of so-called love. What incentive would such then have for true repentance and restoration?

The Example of Ephraim

Consider the way in which God related to Ephraim's deliberate rebellion after repeated pleas from Him. "Ephraim is joined to idols, let him alone" (Hos. 4:17). Yet He keeps the door of hope open in case Ephraim reconsiders his wrong course of being bonded with idols. God hoped against hope that Ephraim would someday see the light and detach himself from his idols and attach himself to Him.

This divine hope for wayward Ephraim is evident in the last chapter of Hosea: "Ephraim shall say, what have I to do anymore with idols?" (Hos. 14:8). God graciously considers any move toward genuine repentance, and He readily responds to it: "I will heal their backsliding, I will love them freely" (v. 4). Notice Christ's counsel in Luke 17:3 in paying close attention to the essential condition of repentance: "Take heed to yourselves. If your brother sins against you, rebuke him; and if he repents, forgive him." Jesus waits and hopes for a genuine turning towards Him, but in His love He does not gloss over our sinful practices but awaits our genuine repentance.

Conditional Forgiveness

The condition for forgiveness still remains to be genuine

repentance. This is crucial to keep in mind today, because they are many so-called Christians who feel totally entitled to forgiveness, carte blanche, without any expression of sorrow, remorse, confession, or repentance. Satan, the great deceiver, has a heyday confusing God's people on this very point of repentance and forgiveness. He "deceives many with the plausible theory that God's love for His people is so great that He will excuse sin in them ... The unconditional pardon of sin never has been, and never will be. . . . The so-called benevolence which would set aside justice is not benevolence but weakness" (*Patriarchs and Prophets*, p. 522).

John, the apostle of love, who knew first hand the true nature of Christ's love, wrote: "But whoever keeps His word, truly the love of God is perfected in him." (1 Jn. 1:5). It is so deceptive and destructive that love, the most beautiful attribute of God's character, is so abused today by the enemy as to excuse evil and justify evil doers. "There are at the present day evils similar to those that threatened the prosperity of the early church, and the teachings of the apostle upon these points should be carefully heeded. 'You must have charity (love),' is the cry to be heard everywhere, especially from those who profess sanctification. But charity is too pure to cover an unconfessed sin. John's teachings are important for those who are living amid the perils of the last days. . . . In this age of boasted liberality these words would be branded as bigotry. But the apostle teaches that while we should manifest Christian courtesy, we are authorized to call sin and sinners by their right names—that this is consistent with true charity" (*The Sanctified Life*, p. 65).

Now look carefully at this striking balance: "While we are to love the souls for whom Christ died, and labor for their salvation, we should not make a compromise with sin. We are not to unite with the rebellious, and call this charity. God requires His people in this age of the world to stand, as did John in his time, unflinchingly for the right, in opposition to soul-destroying errors" (*ibid.*).

While we are to manifest Christian grace and understanding for the intentionally and persistently sinful, we are to care enough to confront such ones with truth spoken in love. This is done for their sake, ours, and the church's as well. Spiritual responsibility is something serious and sacred. Notice what God said through Ezekiel: "When I say to the wicked, 'You shall surely die,' and you give him no warning, nor speak to warn the wicked from his wicked way, to save his life, that same wicked man shall die in his iniquity; but his blood I will require at your hand. Yet, if you warn the wicked and he does not turn from his wickedness, nor from his wicked way, he shall die in his iniquity; but you have delivered your soul." (Ezek. 3:18, 19).

Sobering Counsel

Consider carefully the following balanced and sobering counsel that can help us avoid extremes in dealing with the erring ones:

"Not until you feel that you could sacrifice your own self-dignity, and even lay down your life in order to save an erring brother, have you cast the beam out of your own eye so that you are prepared to help your brother" (*Mount of Blessing*, pp. 128, 129).

"If wrongs are apparent among His people, and if the servants of God pass on indifferent to them, they virtually sustain and justify the sinner, and are alike guilty and will just as surely receive the displeasure of God; for they will be responsible for the sins of the guilty" (*Testimonies*, vol. 3, p. 265).

"The religion which makes of sin a light matter, dwelling on the love of God to the sinner regardless of his actions, only encourages the sinner to believe that God will receive him while he continues in that which he knows to be sin. This is what some are doing who profess to believe present truth. The truth is kept apart from the life, and that is the reason it has no power to convict and convert the soul" (*Testimonies*, vol. 5, p. 540).

DISCUSSION QUESTIONS

1. Try recalling a setback in your life that God used for a comeback. How was this possible? How did such experience enhance a closer walk with Jesus?

2. What does it mean that Christ is praying for you? How does this foster your faith in Him as you confess your sins and seek His forgiveness and restoration?

3. Do you love Jesus more than anyone else, including your family members? Why, or why not?

4. Is there something in your life that you have not yet forgiven yourself of, although you know that God has already forgiven you? What would it take to finally forgive yourself and receive His peace?

5. God's love is unconditional, but all God's promises are conditional. How do you understand this? Do you agree or disagree, and why? Explain: "The unconditional pardon of sin never has been and never will be" (*Patriarchs and Prophets*, p. 522).

6. As we learned, Zacchaeus the tax collector was genuinely repentant, and Jesus forgave and restored him. Some think that if an offending church member deliberately and persistently resists all the steps in Matthew 18, then he should be treated as a tax collector, just as Zacchaeus was treated. What do you think, and why?

CHAPTER EIGHT

Affirming High Expectations

"Let your light so shine before men, that they may see your good
works and glorify your Father in heaven" (Matthew 5:16).
"Therefore you shall be perfect, just as your Father in heaven is
perfect" (Matthew 5:48).

I know of a pastor who always tried to bring his parishioners to a higher spiritual level by his convicting sermons and hearty appeals for revival and reformation. Upon his transition to another district, the pastor was told by one of his church members of how relieved he (the church member) was to hear the news that he was moving to pastor another church. The pastor was puzzled and curious as to why his member felt that way; and he was plainly told that his sermons always pricked his conscience and made him feel uneasy. Apparently this man wanted to come to church and just be comfortable without being called upon to respond to any convicting appeals. He felt that neither the pastor nor his church leaders should have any expectations of him, nor should they hold him accountable for his spiritual development or church involvement. He just wanted to hear things that made him feel good about himself.

The Culture of No Expectations

It seems that the culture of no expectations is gradually

descending upon us. I recently heard someone say to his friend that they should not have any expectations of each other, because in this way neither one would have to deal with any potential letdown or disappointment. This development implies that we are neither here to please or honor anyone, nor are we here to prove ourselves or strive to meet any standards set before us. Before our very own eyes we see education being dumbed down more and more to satisfy the whims of students, and it is becoming old-fashioned to prod anyone to work hard and to strive for excellence, for this may damage one's sense of self-worth, or cause undue stress.

It is likely that the mentality of low or no expectation at all is rooted in a mental defense mechanism. It is supposedly a protective mechanism of our fragile self against any potential disappointment or against offending others. Even though we know that we are created to enjoy human connectedness and expectations, we are sometimes swept along with this notion of low expectation because we want to come across strong and independent like others. We imagine that we are self-sufficient enough not to connect with others or expect anything from them. Thus in denying this God-given need we hope not to be hurt or disappointed.

It is similar to some church members who intentionally join a big church so they can be lost in it without others noticing their comings and goings. They also prefer this situation because they do not have to be held accountable for their actions or for any church responsibility. Their sentiment is that they want to do as they please and be left alone. They do not want any expectations put on them, and if the church seems to go along with them, then maybe God does not expect anything from them either. Sliding down this slippery slope promotes the notion that anything goes, and that whatever good or bad they do is their own prerogative; and no man, not even God can tell them what to do, or hold them accountable. This undermines and even destroys any moral motivation or obligation to put God and others first in our love and service.

God Has Expectations

Yet if we are honest with ourselves we would admit that the resulting hurt or letdown cannot be covered up easily. The plain reason for this outcome is that God created us this way, for He created us in His image. The Bible is replete with moving references to God feeling a letdown, a hurt or a disappointment. We let Him down when we willfully disobey Him, we hurt His heart when we disregard His counsel, and we disappoint Him when He comes expecting fruit but finds only briers. It is normal that any good father would feel this way about his wayward children, simply because he cares.

It is quite apparent in the parable of the vineyard that Christ expected His chosen people to produce fruit, and was greatly disappointed when they did not. Also, in the parable of the talents, He expected the man with one talent to use and increase it, but was disappointed when he went and hid it. Far be it for Christ to have low or no expectations at all; on the contrary, He has high expectations. To the rich young ruler He counseled him to sell all that he had and give to the poor, and then follow Him. This young man would not meet this high expectation because he was very rich. Jesus by no means calls us to an easy religion that accommodates our own selfish inclinations. "Many are deceiving their own souls by living an easy-going, accommodating, crossless religion. But Jesus says, 'If any man will come after Me, let him deny himself, and take up his cross, and follow Me'" (*Selected Messages*, bk. 1, p. 382).

Our Lord exhorts us that if we want to be first, be last; if we want to find our lives then we must lose ourselves in service for others; and if we want to live we must die. This is high expectation indeed! Loving our enemies, and praying for those who despitefully use us is the high goal He sets before each one of us. And when it comes to spreading the gospel, He pushes us to go beyond our comfort zone—from Jerusalem to Judea, Samaria, and to the uttermost parts of the world.

Brother's Keeper

Cain, the first murderer in this world, exemplified this no-expectation mindset. God surely expected him to be his brother's keeper when He asked: "Where is Abel your brother?" But Cain was bothered by such an inquiry of accountability and expectation, apparent in his arrogant response: "I do not know. Am I my brother's keeper?" But the caring heart of God would not be deterred by such a heartless response. "What have you done?" He asked him. "The voice of your brother's blood cries out to me from the ground" (Gen. 4:9, 10).

This no-expectation mindset lives in denial of the incontrovertible truth that all of us are interlinked with the web of humanity. God, who created us in His image and made us all brothers and sisters of His human family, expects us to look out for each other's well-being. And if we refuse to, then the blood-soaked earth will speak, and the stones will cry out. Some excuse the no-expectation posture by advocating that such expectation leads to so-called codependency. But this is a fallacious assumption. Being our brothers' keepers, as our heavenly Father expects of us, does not lead us to relationships of codependency, but to relationships of interdependency. This vital interdependency, which the apostle Paul alludes to in his analogy of the members of the body, causes all church members to work together for the building up of the whole body of Christ.

The other fallacy that excuses this issue of no expectation is the so-called "boundaries," which goes to the extreme of separating and alienating family members and friends from each other under the guise of independence. Now, there is nothing wrong with allowing some breathing space, independence or boundaries—we all need that for sure. But to abuse such an idea in order to detach ourselves from each other, disregarding the bearing of each other's burdens, and looking away from each other's pain and suffering is not at all what God desires. This is nothing short of old-fashioned self-centeredness that says to one's brother your pain is your problem. It has nothing to do with me whatsoever. If my behavior causes you any trouble, then it is none of my business—you deal with it, or get used to it.

This attitude leaves one cold and alone. Once I counseled a young man whose errant conduct caused his parents a lot of grief without ever seeming to care about how they felt. His loving mother suffered a severe heart attack because of all the anxiety and stress he subjected her to. I appealed to his sense of caring for his own mother who had devoted her life to his welfare. His hard response implied that parents should have no expectations of their children, for they should be left free to do whatever they want. I will never forget when he said that his mother's heart attack was totally her problem; and if that led to her demise, it had nothing to do with him—it was her life and it was her death.

God's Ideal for His Children

I was pleasantly surprised recently to be told by one of my students to exhort him to work harder, and to have higher expectations of him. This was in response to my carefulness of not pushing him too harder or possibly offending him. This is not what is usually heard, but it sure sounded right and refreshing to me. My student indicated that placing expectations on him would spur him on to try harder to do his best in fulfilling my high expectations of him. Of course, we do not mean by this that we place too much emphasis on accomplishments and not enough emphasis on unconditional love regardless of accomplishment.

You see, God's love should propel us to do our best in all He wants us to do. But if we carelessly promote low expectation of ourselves and others, then we often find ourselves careless in our relationship to God and His expectations of us. If others do not expect us to do our best, then why should God expect us to rise higher in our spiritual growth? This is such a dangerous development, because we then view God as some indulgent father who showers love on his children without holding them accountable to any standard. This is where overemphasis on God's unconditional love and acceptance leads to a permissive view of behavior. This kind of love and acceptance becomes a subtle and deceptive cover, permitting any desired conduct.

What do you think of this inspired counsel regarding God's high expectation of us? "God's ideal for His children is higher than the highest human thought can reach" (*The Desire of Ages*, p. 311). This sounds like a very high expectation, because He truly believes in our great potential, and He provides sufficient grace to enable us to reach the ideal that He sets before us. The loftiness of heaven and the broadness of the universe are His unlimited aspirations for us. Teachers, pastors, and parents are to cooperate with God is setting high ideals before our youth. "As he [the Christian teacher] awakens a desire to reach God's ideal, he presents an education that is as high as heaven and as broad as the universe; an education that cannot be completed in this life, but will be continued in the life to come" (*Education*, p. 19).

It is important to understand that our Lord does not set a high goal for us to reach on our own, but He inspires and empowers us to pursue excellence as a way of life. This way we never come to a point when we feel we have arrived, but we keep on going forward in His strength, doing better and better. Toyota has an interesting commercial that goes this way: "Striving for excellence is not a goal but a way of life." In other words, the people of the Toyota exist to continually pursue excellence in manufacturing their cars; and no matter how close they come to their goal, they will never sit on their laurels and feel they have arrived.

Doing Our Best

I am grateful that my parents instilled in me this invaluable virtue of always doing my best. They encouraged me in my childhood to not simply get by, to not merely reach a goal, but to always press forward as a way of life. Consequently, throughout the course of my life I have always challenged myself with the question of why not my best in everything I do. For example, I never felt satisfied getting an A grade in an academic course in which I had not done my best; but I felt much better with a B grade if had done my best. And that is what Christ expects of us: by His grace to do our best in following and obeying Him. "When we do our best, He becomes our righteousness" (*Selected Messages*, bk. 1, p. 368). For when we wholeheartedly submit to Him and walk with Him like Enoch, we then become righteous in His righteousness and perfect in His perfection.

In the midst of all these confusing and conflicting trends that we witness all around us, we must ask ourselves the question as to what Jesus expects of us. In His great love for us, does He have high expectations of us? What kind of expectations and how such expectations affect our relationship with Him? Consider the following two powerful examples to illustrate the height and depth which Christ inspires us to reach, believing that we can do all things through Him who strengthens us.

Perfect in His Perfection

"Therefore you shall be perfect, just as your Father in heaven is perfect" (Matt. 5:48). Our heavenly Father's perfection is absolute in His divine sphere, just as by His grace our perfection is relative in our human sphere. "Relative" is referring to our Christian perfection which is never static or absolute, but continuously growing and maturing. And this dynamic process of human perfection starts here and continues in heaven for eternity. In relationship to our heavenly Father, we "may be perfect in our sphere, even as God is perfect in His" (*Mount of Blessing*, p. 77). And in relationship to our Savior: "As the Son of Man was perfect in His life, so His followers are to be perfect in their life" (*The Desire of Ages*, p. 311).

In a similar way, Christ calls on us to be "the light of the world" (Matt. 5:14), even though He is the perfect and absolute light of the universe. We are indeed darkness in ourselves, but in His light we become light. "We are to be centers of light and blessing to our little circle, even as He is to the universe. We have nothing of ourselves, but the light of His love shines upon us, and we are to reflect its brightness" (*My Life Today*, p. 38). Of course, we cannot equal the excellency of Christ because He is beyond all comparison, but He reaches us where we are, graciously adapts His life to our human condition in order for us to imitate Him in our sphere. "We cannot gain and possess the influence that He [Christ] had; but why should we not educate ourselves to come just as near to the Pattern as it is possible for us to do?" (*Testimonies*, vol. 2, p. 618).

"I Never Knew You"

The other example of Christ's high expectation is how He views our intimate relationship with Him. "Not everyone who says to Me, 'Lord, Lord,' shall enter the kingdom of heaven, but he who does the will of My Father in heaven. Many will say to Me in that day, 'Lord, Lord, have we not prophesied in Your name, cast out demons in Your name, and done many wonders in Your name?' And then I will declare to them, 'I never knew you; depart from Me, you who practice lawlessness!'" (Matt. 7:22, 23). It is quite evident here that our Lord is not at all impressed with mere profession of His name, or even of great accomplishments in His name. He does not want us to simply profess His name with our mouth, but more importantly, He desires us to possess Him in our hearts.

Only with such personal possession of the heart can we be fruitful in doing the will of His Father, and consequently enter His kingdom. He holds in high regard this indispensable, personal relationship with Him. This relationship goes way beyond mere empty claims and posturing. Nothing is hid from Him, for He knows well the deep intent of our hearts, and is keenly aware if we truly know Him or not. We may even accomplish great feats in His name and go as far as prophesying, casting out demons, and doing many wonders without really knowing Him personally. In fact, we may find ourselves so distracted by our great accomplishments that we are not attracted to the one thing that is needed—for Him to know us personally as intimate friends.

The bottom line is this: Christ wants to know us, and He wants us to know Him intimately as loving and loyal friends. Then out of this intimate friendship, good works and great accomplishments proceed. Such works and accomplishments, even in His name, do not and will never substitute for the priority of this intimate friendship. We will never make it to His glorious kingdom and enjoy intimate fellowship there unless we are learning to be intimate friends with Him here. We must consider seriously the following questions in view of our eternal destiny: Do we love Jesus more than anyone or anything else? Is He the first and foremost priority in our daily lives? If so, do we yearn to spend intimate time with Him daily in order for our friendship with Him to thrive? Listen to what He said about this priority upon His heart: "He who loves father or mother more than Me is not worthy of Me. And he who loves son or daughter more than Me is not worthy of Me" (Matt. 10:37).

Some so-called "friends" reach out to us only when they need us to do something for them; but if nothing is needed, then they do not bother to keep the friendship alive. Is this how we treat Jesus as we claim He is our Friend? We go to Him only when we are in trouble, and not because we cherish out time together with Him. Is our first and foremost priority right now, as His coming draws near, to do our utmost best to be the closest to Him? In that day when Jesus comes again, our fancy words and our impressive accomplishments in His name will not matter. Only His words that He knows us and the invitation to enter His kingdom will matter then. But if we are distracted now from knowing Him, under the guise of being too busy doing good things, then on that day He will have to declare the painful truth: "I never knew you; depart from Me, you who practice lawlessness!" (Matt. 7:23). We must stare this reality straight in the face, for this is exactly what is going to happen in the final analysis.

Built to Last

It is interesting to note that Christ immediately follows up His declaration in the judgment by saying, "I never knew you . . ." with the parables about the house built on rock and the other built on sand. He closely associates the experience of hearing His words *and* doing them with the wise man who anchored his house on bedrock. Often we see shallow house foundations dug and cement poured without reaching bedrock, and that is why there is settling and shifting of the soil, and even cracking of the walls. I grew up in the Bible lands where builders keep on digging, so the foundations of buildings will be anchored on solid bedrock.

This solid bedrock, where our lives are securely established, is Jesus. This is where we find the harmonious integration of hearing and doing, loving and obeying, and having that living faith that works by love. This is the opposite of practicing lawlessness, for it is the power of the gospel to transform our lives and to make us one in Christ. The ideal condition for our love relationship is to have nothing between our soul and our Savior—no sinking sand, no shifting soil—but only our anchor to our Lord, the bedrock. John, the apostle of love, defined precisely and unambiguously what genuine love is when he wrote: "For this is the love of God, that we keep His commandments. And His commandments are not burdensome" (1 Jn. 5:3). This genuine love that always leads to obedience is the bedrock of our relationship with Jesus, and this is what He ardently desires for each one of us.

The two houses Jesus refers to appear the same on the surface. The foundations of rock and sand beneath are not readily seen. But when the crises of torrential rains descend, the surging floods threaten, and the angry winds howl, then true character is revealed. True character is the unvarnished truth which Jesus knows about our innermost souls. It is not so much what people think about us, it is what He thinks of us. This is what He means by knowing us: it is that solid and intimate relationship with Him that has nothing to do with any pretension or presumption. There is too much "sand" in our relationships with others, and precious little bedrock. That is why the saying is true that genuine friendships are tested and revealed through crises.

Love Used As Camouflage

Satan, the great deceiver, loves to camouflage his deceptive ways under the guise of so-called "love." The love that is misguided, self-centered, and irresponsible. It is quite a popular subject with him, and he loves to talk to people about it in order to subtly deceive them. And he is extremely successful at this, and many are swept away by such talk of love in our permissive age. He certainly has refined his expertise on this subject—especially in our relationship with God and others—as long as he presents it in a counterfeit way. He deftly uses such a cover-up to entice people into sensuality, immorality, permissiveness, and lack of accountability—all under the guise of love.

But genuine love is diametrically different. This is what it is about, and the profound impact it has in the life: "Those who have genuine love for God will manifest an earnest desire to *know* His will and to *do* it." For example, "The child who loves his parents will show that love by willing obedience; but the selfish, ungrateful child seeks to do as little as possible for his parents, while he is at the same time desires to enjoy all the privileges granted to the obedient and faithful" (*The Sanctified Life*, p. 81, emphasis supplied).

And now for the spiritual application for all of us: "The same difference is seen among those who profess to be children of God. Many who know that they are the objects of His love and care, and who desire to receive His blessings, take no delight in doing His will. They regard His claims upon them as unpleasant restraint, His commandments as grievous yoke. But he who is truly seeking for holiness of heart and life delights in the law of God, and mourns only that he fails so far short of meeting its requirements" (*ibid.*).

Heart Service Not Lip Service

Christ's high expectations for us are possible because He supplies all the grace needed to help us reach His ideal. He is never satisfied with lip service, but He is delighted in heart service. When we love Him halfheartedly and selfishly, He calls us to love Him wholeheartedly and selflessly. Look at how much He believes in us and the high potential He sees in us if we open our hearts to His empowering grace. Jesus said: "You shall love the Lord your God with all your heart, with all your soul, and with all your mind" (Matt. 22:37). He believes we can love Him with all our being; and how delightful and honorable this is that we may through Him attain this high level of a close relationship.

The bedrock for loving God with all our being is this, that Christ loves us with all His being as the Father has loved Him. "And the Father loved Me, I also have loved you; abide in My love" (Jn. 15:9). And He expects us to love each other with the same love He showers upon us. "This is My commandment, that you love one another as I have loved you. Greater love has no one than this, than to lay down one's life for his friends" (Jn. 15:12, 13). His high hope for us is to love Him supremely and to love others selflessly and sacrificially. Our enemies must also be included in those we love. "For if you love those who love you," Jesus said, "what reward have you?" (Matt. 5:46). This high level of love can only spring forth from a grateful heart for God's unconditional love. Such love is an invariable principle that is not conditioned by fleeting feelings or changeable circumstances, but is the overflow of a regenerate heart.

"When love fills the heart, it will flow out to others, not because of favors received from them, but because love is the principle of action" (*Mount of Blessing*, p. 38). Moreover, "To be kind to the unthankful and to the evil, to do good hoping for nothing again, is the insignia of the royalty of heaven . . ." (*Ibid*, p. 75). It was taught during Christ's time to love friends and hate enemies. That is why He took this corrective measure: "But I say to you, love your enemies, bless those who curse you, do good to those who hate you, and pray for those who spitefully use you and persecute you" (Matt. 5:44).

Affirming High Expectations

"Love Your Enemies"

Sometime ago I was watching a television call-in show in which an angry Muslim clergy was castigating a former Muslim who had converted to Christ. The clergyman was reviling and cursing this poor convert, and was saying all manner of evil against him. What really impressed me was the calm and loving response in the face of such vitriol. I will never forget what the convert said to him: "Sir, if you wish to keep on cursing and reviling me for being a Christian, then I will do the loving thing Jesus told me do: to bless you and thus be blessed. So the more you revile me the more He blesses me." The upset clergyman had no idea how to fight against such unconditional Christian love, so in frustration he simply hung up. (See also Matt. 5:11). How can anyone conquer such a true disciple of Jesus! What weapons would anyone deploy against such a Christian if such weapons only bring blessings upon him!

The Jesus who taught His disciples to love even their enemies, Himself loved His bitterest enemies. In His dying agony on the cross, He deeply loved and earnestly prayed for those whose hearts were totally calloused toward Him: "Father, forgive them, for they do not know what they do" (Lk. 23:34). And He was dead serious about His Father answering His earnest pleas for His tormentors. In spite of a seemingly hopeless situation, He harbored the high hope and extravagant expectation for them to repent and be forgiven. It is so amazing but so true that His fervent prayers were answered in their behalf! Many of those rabble-rousers were cut to the heart and repented at the Pentecostal preaching of Peter and his fellow apostles. (See *The Acts of the Apostles*, pp. 42-44).

Infinite Possibilities

This is what it really means to be genuine followers of Jesus. In their lives they reveal that they are being transformed into a higher and still higher level of Christlikeness. In their lives the promise is fulfilled that "all things work together for good to those who love God, to those who are the called according to His purpose" (Rom. 8:28). In all His teachings Jesus expected His hearers to do better and better and to rise higher and higher in whatever He called them to do. And He desires us today to advance forward and upward, to become the head and not the tail. His highest joy is to work with the rejects of society and that through His power they can become the best. To be a "Christian is to be Christlike. Jesus is a perfect pattern, and we must imitate His example. A Christian is the highest type of man, a representative of Christ" (*Evangelism*, p. 641).

He longs to work on the hopeless, despised, despairing, and the seemingly worthless and bring them up with Him to a higher level. "In every human being, however fallen, He beheld a son of God, one who might be restored to the privilege of His divine relationship. . . . In every human being He discerned infinite possibilities. He saw men as they might be, transfigured by His grace. . . . Looking upon them with hope, He inspired hope. Meeting them with confidence, He inspired trust. Revealing in Himself man's true ideal, He awakened, for its attainment, both desire and faith. In His presence souls despised and fallen realized that they still were men, and they longed to prove themselves worthy of His regard. In many a heart that seemed dead to all things holy, were awakened new impulses. To many a despairing one there opened the possibility of a new life." (*Education*, pp. 79, 80).

To take wretched beings and retrace His image in them, to bring them up higher as a showcase of His transforming power is what brings Him honor and glory. To valiantly fight for each soul ensnared by Satan's chains, and to decisively defeat him on his own turf is a powerful testament before the whole universe. The parable of the lost coin recorded in Luke 15:8-10 is a good example here. Although it was defaced with encrustations of rust and rubbish, yet Christ was intent on recovering the luster of His divine image and superscription in that seemingly hopeless coin. This is similar to what is recorded in Zechariah 3:2. These "brands plucked from the fire" will become precious jewels in Christ's crown—the closest and dearest to His heart.

Turning Defeat into Victory

Fellow believer, no matter how bleak the circumstances seem to be at present, "Press with determination in the right direction, and circumstances will be your helpers, not your hindrances.... Thus you turn defeat into victory, disappointing the enemy and honoring your Redeemer" (*Christ's Object Lessons*, p. 332). And the ultimate victory will be the salvation of those who are like "brands plucked from the fire," and who have been wrestled from the deadly clutches of Satan. Look at Mary whom Christ delivered seven times from the bondage of demon possession. She became one of His closest followers in this world, and will be so in heaven.

What a powerful testimony before the whole universe to the high hope Christ placed in her potential! This also applies to the ones who were the closest to Satan, who now through God's power become the closest to Jesus. "Nearest the throne are those who were once zealous in the cause of Satan, but who plucked as brands from the burning, have followed their Savior with deep, intense devotion. Next are those who perfected Christian characters in the midst of falsehood and infidelity, those who honored the law of God ... and the millions, of all ages, who were martyred for their faith" (*The Great Controversy*, p. 665).

Consider how Christ encouraged Peter in various difficult circumstances to reach higher and still higher. Even though He knew that Peter was going to deny Him three times, He held out renewed hope that he was going to repent and then strengthen his brethren (Lk. 22:32). Later on when Peter felt that he was perhaps not dependable enough to shepherd Christ's flock, Christ commissioned him three times to feed His lambs and sheep (Jn. 21:15-17). Moreover, Christ trusted him enough to deem him worthy of the highest honor of being crucified for Him. The same Peter who pledged to die with Him before the whole nation, played the coward before a servant girl, and denied that he ever knew Him. Jesus spoke these parting words regarding Peter's future martyrdom. He would have never uttered these words to Peter if He had not had the highest hope and expectation for him.

"Most assuredly, I say to you, when you were younger, you girded yourself and walked where you wished; but when you are old, you will stretch out your hands, and another will gird you and carry you where you do not wish." This He spoke, signifying by what death he would glorify God . . ." (Jn. 21:18, 19). Although Peter proved to be a formidable champion for Christ, he was eager to prove Himself to Jesus by paying the ultimate sacrifice for His cause. He did not have to, but he was ever anxious to clearly demonstrate his ultimate love and loyalty to His beloved Master.

Surely Peter ever remembered the sincere pledge he made to Jesus, but he could not then keep it. "Even if I have to die with You," Peter vowed, "I will not deny You!" (Matt. 26:35). He now finally had the chance of a lifetime to fulfill his pledge of being crucified for his Lord. "Peter, as a Jew and a foreigner, was condemned to be scourged and crucified. In prospect of his fearful death, the apostle remembered his great sin in denying Jesus in the hour of His trial. Once so unready to acknowledge the cross, he now counted it a joy to yield up his life for the gospel, feeling only that, for him who had denied his Lord, to die in the same manner as His Master died was too great an honor.

Peter had sincerely repented of that sin and had been forgiven by Christ. . . . But he could never forgive himself. Not even the thought of the agonies of the last terrible scene could lessen the bitterness of his sorrow and repentance. As a last favor he entreated the executioners that he might be nailed to the cross with his head downward. The request was granted, and in this manner died the great apostle Peter" (*The Acts of the Apostles*, pp. 537, 538).

Certainly the highest expectation of Christ for each one of us is that He longs to have us become like Him in reflecting His character. He yearns to have us be prepared as His pure bride when He comes to take us to the homes He has prepared for us. His highest hope for us is that He will entrust us with heaven as His faithful and loyal disciples, to share in His glory for eternity. It does not get any better than that! May each one of us, by His empowering grace, fulfill His high expectations in our lives as we journey through this world with Him, and soon journey with Him in the world to come. Maranatha!

DISCUSSION QUESTIONS

1. What do you think brought about the mindset of low expectations? How can a mindset of high expectations in our love and service to Christ be restored?

2. How would you explain and apply this inspired comment? "God's ideal for His children is higher than the highest human thought can reach" (*The Desire of Ages*, p. 311).

3. How do you explain relative perfection as it relates to us, and absolute perfection as it relates to God? When we submit to and walk with Jesus, we become perfect in His perfection. What does this assertion mean to you?

4. In what ways do you think your character is built on solid bedrock or on shifting sand? What difference does your

answer make in your Christian walk?

5. Do you remember when Jesus helped you turn defeat into victory? What are some high goals you would like to reach in serving Christ, but feeling so inadequate? How can God's abundant grace help you in this process?

Christ's Way
to
RESTORATION

Philip G. Samaan

The message of John the Baptist who is "the Elijah to come" must be the message of the final remnant: a message of true repentance and restoration to prepare the way for Christ's second coming. Lucifer plunged our world into the abyss of brokenness and alienation impacting every sphere of human existence. But Christ's divine strategy is to overwhelm and defeat Satan's deceptive designs and to bring about ultimate healing and restoration.

Christ's Way of Reaching People

Philip G. Samaan

The Fine Art of Relational Witnessing

The focus is on the fine art of relational witnessing. It presents the six steps of Christ's way of reaching people, and how we may successfully model such steps in our daily lives. The book is punctuated with numerous illustrations and experiences to make it easy to apply.

Christ's Way to Spiritual Growth

Author of *Christ's Way of Reaching People*

Philip G. Samaan

Christian spirituality is the dynamic process of becoming Christlike. The emphasis in this book is on modeling Christ's example of true spirituality in such a way that people who interact with us take notice that we have been with Jesus.

Christ's Way
of Making Disciples

Philip G. Samaan

Author of *Christ's Way of Reaching People*
and *Christ's Way to Spiritual Growth*

The urgent need of the church today is not merely to win converts, but to reproduce and multiply fruitful disciples. This book explores the dynamic process and progressive steps of Christ's approach of transforming us and others into fruit-bearing disciples.

How Christ Prays For Us and With Us

Christ's Way to Pray

Philip G. Samaan

Author of Christ's Way to Restoration, Christ's Way to Spiritual
Growth, Christ's Way of Reaching People,
and Christ's Way of Making Disciples

Christ's Way to Pray explains that the answer to prevailing prayer is not found in focusing on our prayers, but in joining our weak prayers with Christ's mighty prayers—the Christ who passionately and perpetually prays for us and with us.

Christ longs to take our "smelly" prayers and fragrance them with the "much incense" of His prayers.

As you linger in the embrace of the praying Jesus, let Him encircle you with His compassionate human arm. And with His mighty divine arm, let Him grasp the throne of God.